VOYAGES

SIDETRACKED BEYOND

Sidetracked

gestalten

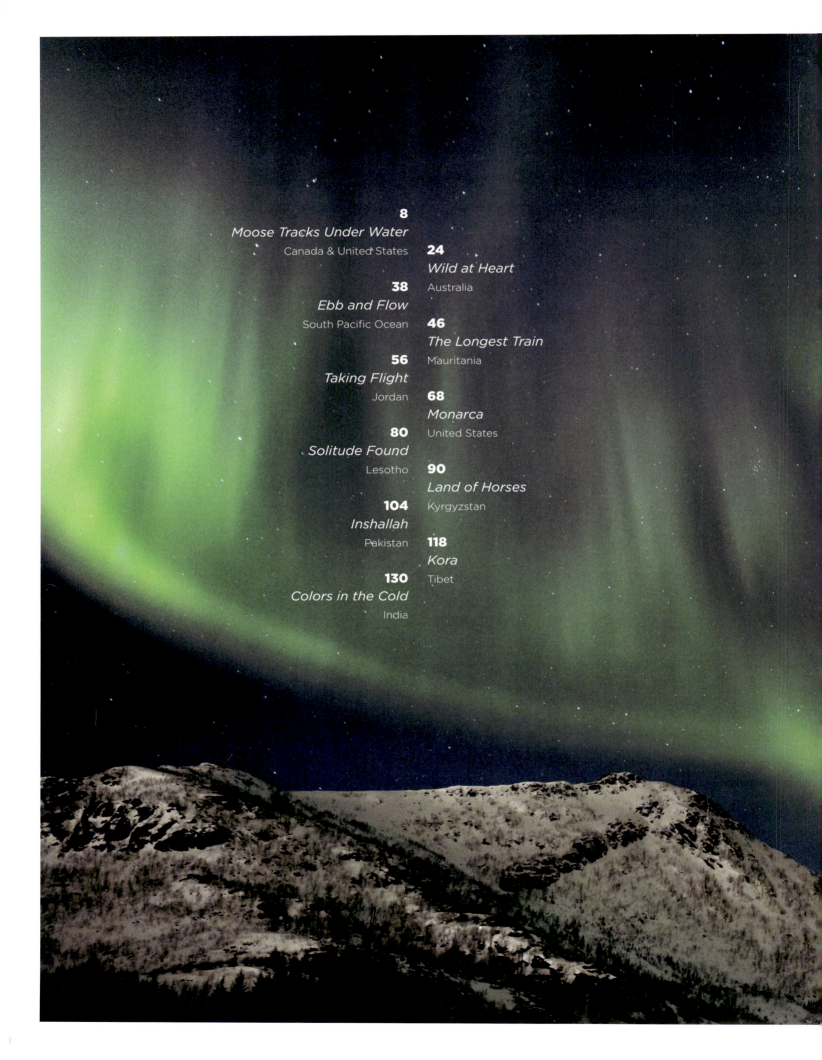

8
Moose Tracks Under Water
Canada & United States

24
Wild at Heart
Australia

38
Ebb and Flow
South Pacific Ocean

46
The Longest Train
Mauritania

56
Taking Flight
Jordan

68
Monarca
United States

80
Solitude Found
Lesotho

90
Land of Horses
Kyrgyzstan

104
Inshallah
Pakistan

118
Kora
Tibet

130
Colors in the Cold
India

142
The Dream Line
Tajikistan

156
Sounds of Silence
Japan

170
Kingdom of Spirits
Greenland

180
Forever Dreaming
Iceland

194
Vintage Souls
Iceland

204
The Colbalt Void
Greenland

218
The Four Rules
Iceland

230
Reconnection
Faroe Islands

244
Through the Ragnarök Fires
Iceland

256
Circle of the Sun
Norway

PREFACE
The Journey Makes the Story

BY JENNY TOUGH

No matter their duration or distance, the longest journeys can have the power to change us in ways that we can scarcely imagine at the start. I have always promoted the idea that adventure is a mindset, and no other qualifications are necessary. A daily dog walk can become an adventure if you are willing to make believe. That said, there is something immensely special about human-powered, long-distance journeys through nature.

Through the lens of endurance sports, where I enjoy pushing my own personal limitations physically and mentally, I have enjoyed traveling the world—thereby expanding my mind and heart in countless ways. There is a magical crossover between travel and endurance. From competing in ultra cycling races in remote terrain, to unsupported solo crossings of mountain ranges on every continent, I have been inspired to push my boundaries and see the world from a unique perspective. In moving through these landscapes by human power, I have experienced so much more than the tourist bus could ever show me. Long-distance journeys can reveal both the world and our own selves in new ways we never imagined.

There is a sense of achievement that comes from reaching journey's end through your own sweat and determination. It can hardly be compared to anything in a comfortable life. Whether walking, paddling, skiing, riding, or sliding, the fortitude it takes to commit yourself—every day—to moving forward, sometimes against the elements or your own better judgment, is immeasurable. Through these long journeys we meet ourselves in intense clarity. We find our strengths and weaknesses and spend hours alongside them on the trail, contemplating our own character and the purpose we bring. We look inside ourselves and also around ourselves, and through this transformative journey we grow—often in ways that build us beyond our own previously held self-image. This is why long journeys become so life-altering for those who take part.

Trek the frozen Zanskar River in Ladakh. Find solitude by mountain bike in Lesotho. Listen to the sounds of silence while ski touring in Japan. Seek remote surf on the Hornstrandir peninsula. Reconnect with the art of solo travel in the Faroe Islands. Sail the seas of the Arctic. Help Indigenous biologists conserve moose in Minnesota and Ontario. Take a T2 camper van to Iceland. Meet Buddhist monks in Tibet. Or soar the length of the USA by paraglider, tracing the migratory route of the monarch butterfly.

To take on a journey like this, to be willing to meet yourself in this clarity, and then to tell a story and capture images to inspire or educate others, is a special gift. At Sidetracked, we believe deeply in the power of storytelling to make a difference for the lives that share this wonderful planet of ours. In these pages, we have selected some of our favorite stories from long-distance journeys around the world—stories that in many cases have been adapted from our critically acclaimed print journal. Those who created these stories hold a wide range of perspectives, but are united in their passion for adventure with a purpose. I hope that through enjoying their stories your imagination will be sparked for your next journey.

Jenny Tough is an adventurer, endurance athlete, and writer.
She is Sidetracked's deputy editor.

"Seek out the undiscovered.
Journey with passion
and purpose. Open eyes to see the
world—differently.
Share meaningful, authentic stories
that represent all life
on this planet. Because by creating
an inspiring community, together
we can forge a trail for positive change."

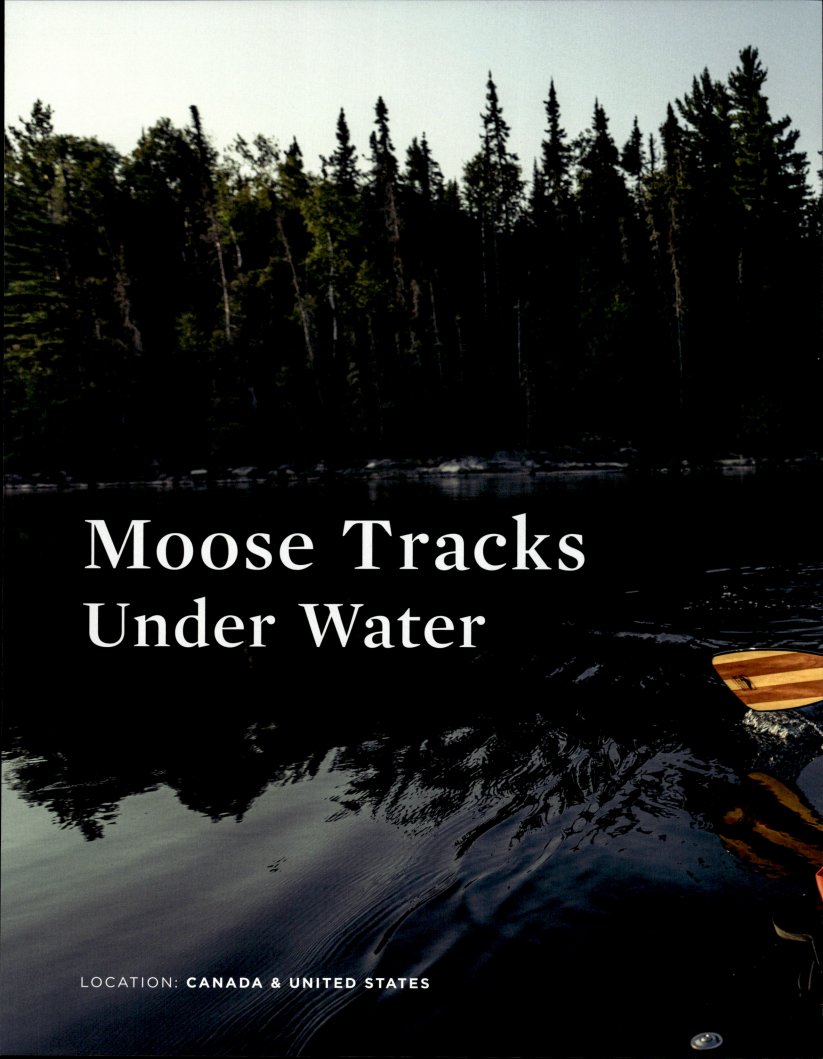

Moose Tracks Under Water

LOCATION: **CANADA & UNITED STATES**

In 2023, photographer and writer Ian Finch embarked on a canoe expedition seeking to understand why the moose is declining catastrophically in Ontario and Minnesota. The aim was to film and photograph the moose in their natural habitat, and connect with Indigenous biologist Seth Moore as they paddled through southern Ontario and northern Minnesota, learning about ecosystem health and potential issues revolving around the second-largest land mammal in North America.

Seth, as lead biologist for the Indigenous community—the Grand Portage Band of Chippewa (Ojibwe)—aimed to sustain the species at a healthy level for the annual subsistence moose hunt, which the Band had been conducting for centuries.

Seth, fellow Indigenous biologists, and his colleagues within the Band protected the moose for their ancestral right to hunt and gather sustainably. In a bid to understand, from a deeper scientific and Indigenous perspective, what is being done to help this magical species survive, Ian launched a multi-year project.

"Around the fires each night, eating fish caught by rod and line, they listened to the haunting sound of loons echoing around the night-time lake systems. Nearby packs of wolves howled; the team howled back from the shoreline. Seth, with his deep knowledge of the terrain and its natural inhabitants, estimated they were surrounded by two packs of wolves."

It began with a 10-day canoe journey into a remote wilderness area, reported to contain healthy moose—but in low numbers. Accompanying them were filmmaker Jamie Barnes from the UK, and expedition canoeist Martin Trahan from Québec.

At the pontoon in a small bay surrounded by dense forest, Ian and Jamie loaded up into the first float plane. Canoes were strapped tightly beside the flotation runners. Seth and Martin had loaded into the second plane, and would land roughly 30 minutes after they had chosen a suitable landing point and called in its location. This spot, 100 kilometers (62 miles) southwest, was a lake that had not been landed by pilots before. From there they would travel northeast through swamp systems, taking on lengthy portages between lake and island regions back to a quiet pickup point close to the original start location.

One hour later, Ian watched with Jamie from a remote sandy beach as their plane thundered into the distance behind a wall of vaporized water produced by the engine thrust. "That's it, he's gone—let's wait for the boys," Jamie remarked as he positioned his camera on the tripod. As a final acknowledgement, the pilot circled back over in a low pass, dipping his wing, to ensure they knew they were alone from this moment.

The second plane with Seth and Martin appeared in the distance, and it too circled over at low altitude to survey conditions before putting down. Within the hour, their canoes were on the water, and they pushed upstream through small rivers interlinking the vast peppered lake systems of this wilderness area. Over lunch, Martin mentioned how quiet, wild, and remote this region felt. But they were in it together. It was the scale and grandeur that made them feel so impermanent and small.

Along the initial northeasterly phase of their route, they paddled into the quietest marshy corners at dawn and dusk, carefully choosing each bay for its potential access route for moose or likelihood of suitable habitat. They were looking for the swamp and flooded high grass areas: places moose would frequent on their morning or evening routines. During these moments of recce, lake system after lake system, one end to the other, they would look for flattened camp spots on raised areas above the dark Ontario waters. There they would regroup, laugh around the fire, and sip from Minnesota whiskey Seth had brought to add a wholesome warmth to the cold windy evenings.

"The footprints, Ian began to feel,
were of ghosts unseen."

> "All these are the potential reasons moose are on the decline, but fundamentally a warming climate is at the heart of this issue."

Day after day, they probed and paddled into motionless swampy bays cloaked in mist. Seth fashioned a moose call from a white bleach bottle, and let out strategic low nasal calls as they sat motionless under the squalls of drizzle sweeping through. The echoes from Seth's mimic call reverberated like a bouncing ball in the immediate area. As he called louder, aiming to reach moose deeper within the miles of impenetrable forest, the calls would reach further out only to echo back to the drifting canoes. They waited for the return call of a nearby bull or cow. Each time, silence would be the only response. The landscape appeared desperately empty.

In the shallow waters of each swampy bay, Seth whispered to Ian, "Moose tracks under water!"—a sign that they were close to a notable crossing point and frequented local habitat. But the repetition of call and silence permeated each morning paddle into the tangerine colors of sunrise. The same routine played out each evening too, paddling in a quiet and undisturbed corner of Ontario sunset. The footprints, Ian began to feel, were of ghosts unseen.

Jamie, glued to his high-powered binoculars, surveyed for movement after each call. "The constant searching, it's exhausting," he would remark. Yet he continued—meticulously, hour after hour, minute after minute. Martin, by contrast, enjoyed the vast wilderness stretching out from each lakeshore as he paddled, the smile on his face difficult to subdue.

Around the fires each night, eating fish caught by rod and line, they listened to the haunting sound of loons echoing around the night-time lake systems. Nearby packs of wolves howled; the team howled back from the shoreline. Seth, with his deep knowledge of the terrain and its natural inhabitants, estimated they were surrounded by two packs of wolves. The following day, during a long portage between two lakes, Ian uncovered wolf scat. Seth inspected it closely, pronouncing it two to four days old and containing moose calf hair.

In moments like this, Seth moved from seasoned canoeist to deeply knowledgeable biologist, sharing the grim but all-too-familiar story of what he felt was unfolding for the moose. When Seth spoke, the others would sit on canoe barrels or lean on paddles, listening intently. "In recent years," he said, "warming winters have allowed white-tailed deer to migrate north into the territory of the moose. Wolves follow the deer north, only to discover the easier pickings of moose calves. The deer bring a brain worm that infects the moose, creating a lack of sensory perception, deafness, and ultimately paralysis. Alongside this, ticks now survive as winters continue to warm. Moose have been found with over 100,000 ticks attached. All these are the potential reasons moose are on the decline, but fundamentally a warming climate is at the heart of this issue."

The team sat in silence as Seth spoke, like students and a professor. His insight, care, and passion energized Jamie and Ian to make sure every stone would be turned, every voice heard, every perspective given—especially Indigenous, conservation, and protection voices. At the time of the expedition in 2023, moose were listed as a Species of Concern due to their disappearance in northern Minnesota, but were not yet considered endangered.

After nine days and nights, the team limped tiredly into their final pull-out location. No moose were sighted. They felt disheartened but not discouraged. Thoughts of warm showers, clean hands, and a soft bed rushed Ian through packing up and portaging to the waiting vehicle location—then back to a rented lakeside cabin for the night. There they went over the choices they had made. Although every effort to see one of these immense animals had been in vain, every second had been worth it nonetheless.

Before Seth left for the US, he and Ian shared logistics and ideas for the next stage of the project. This would be the first round of many interviews with Seth, other biologists, and—crucially—members of the Grand Portage Band. These perspectives would help Ian and Jamie uncover what was to come in terms of understanding and protecting this beautiful species.

Wild at Heart

LOCATION: **AUSTRALIA**

Running for over 5,330 kilometers (3,312 miles) down the spine of eastern Australia, the Bicentennial National Trail is one of the longest walking trails in the world. In 2016, Alienor Le Gouvello set out to complete this journey with three horses: Cooper, River, and Roxanne. Since the trail's inception in 1988, only 35 people had completed it—but no one with wild horses, and only one other woman alone. More people had walked on the moon. The trail began with a ruggedly beautiful but isolated section. This dry country, with chalk-white and ocher rocks rising up all around them, was harsh on the horses' feet—and difficult for them to negotiate, laden as they were with heavy gear. There were river crossings. Huge eucalyptus forests. After a few days, it felt as though she was in the middle of the remote bush. But, despite these challenges, she also felt free.

Leading three horses across the high Victorian country proved complicated. If one pulled back, then the others were at risk too, especially on sheer, scree-ridden sections. And in the beginning there was always one pulling back, unresponsive to Alienor's guidance. The two boys, Cooper and River, were not up for it; they would plant their feet in the ground and refuse to move as she attempted to lead them on foot. Dragging them up and down exposed mountain trails was a killer. Each time they reached a summit, or the crest of a pass, joy faded as she saw the summit of the next in the distance.

"The horses were her priority. She always took care of them first, washing them down before making camp. Building a fireplace with rocks and logs, she would picture the place as her home, then pitch the tent and corral the horses for the night."

Her two boys might have been trained, but they did not start with the right work ethic, and one thought was dominant in Alienor's mind: *If they are behaving like stubborn mules now, how the hell can we do 5,000 kilometers like this?* Cursing, and hurling the lead ropes to the ground, Alienor would fall to her feet to weep.

At last, in the middle of one hot day, exhausted and frustrated, Alienor looked to her mare, Roxanne—loving her in that moment for her patience and stamina— and told her, "Girl, you've got to help me. This really isn't working." So Alienor put a leather knee hobble around her neck and tied the two boys to her. For days she pulled them up and down the mountains until eventually they understood— they were not getting out of this. Soon they were charging up and down the trails, working as a team.

Every day, Alienor found a home for them in the bush: somewhere that would offer shade, good grass, water. The horses were her priority. She always took care of them first, washing them down before making camp. Building a fireplace with rocks and logs, she would picture the place as her home, then pitch the tent and corral the horses for the night. When finally sitting on her sheepskin to eat something, the horses would graze around her, nudging her on the shoulder wanting some of whatever she was eating. Roxanne would lick her bowl for the remains of her porridge. They lived camp life together.

Each night, the horses' bells would be Alienor's reassurance; when she did not hear them she would worry. So, when the hunters came, she feared for them as though they were her children. Far more than she feared for herself.

It was within a state forest, quite early on, when the three hunters came. Alienor had been traveling with an old rider and his horses—a kind stranger who had helped her through a mountainous section. Firelight washed their world with its warm glow. The hunters were in their late forties, early fifties, and spoke to each other in a Slavic language. Alienor could not tell what they were saying. One wore old-school yellow Aviator sunglasses, and they were covered in guns, bullets, knives, military gear; one gripped a long leash, hauling back a nasty looking pit-bull. Foam spat from its mouth as it growled and barked, furious and savage. They parked right next to Alienor and the old rider, and bragged about what they had killed—on the roof of their trucks were the bloodied, broken bodies of dingoes and snakes.

The hunters walked around their camp, looking at their gear. Alienor and the old rider tried to stay pleasant. She did not tell them what she was doing there, a woman trekking a trail like this; they simply said they would be leaving in the morning. Although Alienor camped a little away from the old guy, both slept with one eye open that night, trying to discern from the slightest sound whether someone was interfering with their corral.

"Flood waters made filtering water difficult; pools and rivers were murky and most had been stagnant for weeks, soiled by rotting cow carcasses."

When dawn came, Alienor set about breaking camp to leave them behind. It was one of the few times she felt vulnerable.

The second time was on top of a mountain pass. Alienor was asleep in her tent when she was woken by Cooper, snorting to indicate that he felt threatened. Unzipping her tent, she saw torchlight. Three men, rowdy and drunk, were harassing the horses in their corral. It was the middle of the night; the middle of nowhere. If she had come out, if she had revealed she was a woman on her own… well, she had heard things could happen out here. So she took out her knife and waited, terrified. It went on for more than an hour. Eventually, they left having not even seen her tent.

After coming so far, crossing all types of terrain in every kind of weather, all it took to bring her down was a single mosquito.

That March, Severe Tropical Cyclone Debbie became the deadliest cyclone to hit Australia in 40 years. It devastated over 1,000 kilometers (621 miles) of coast with extreme winds and flash floods, killing 14 people. Floodwater left the trail ravaged: trees ripped up, bridges splintered and wrecked, heaving rivers impassable on horseback. At the Burdekin Dam wall, Alienor was forced to pull up for days and wait for the water level to drop. The stagnant water and increased humidity meant there were also a lot more mosquitoes.

Flood waters made filtering water difficult; pools and rivers were murky and most had been stagnant for weeks, soiled by rotting cow carcasses. Alienor would filter her water carefully through a cloth at first, then through her filter several times, and finally drink through a LifeStraw. During one of these laborious exercises, crouching beside a stagnant pool, a mosquito bit her.

For a week she struggled with worsening symptoms—fever, rash, extreme pain in the joints—barely covering the distance she needed to.

Every step an agonizing misery. Only later did she learn that this febrile, shivering, burning nightmare was called Ross River Fever, a repulsive sibling of Dengue Fever.

River and Cooper had pulled back at the start, recalcitrant and defiant. Now they were the ones pulling Alienor on and supporting her. But she knew it could not continue. As Roxanne voiced her concern, watching her through dark, expressive eyes, Alienor knew she had responsibilities. She was camping on the other side of the Burdekin Dam, in a remote place with nowhere secure to leave her horses. She needed to see to them before she could take care of herself.

The only place she could find cell service was at the top of a hill. Every step to reach it was agony. As she lay in her shelter, she remembered a young woman she had spoken to who had a ranch nearby. Through interference and poor signal, she managed to call her, and the woman gave Alienor directions to the ranch—although a long ride, it was possible.

Dosed up on painkillers, Alienor saddled up Roxanne and they rode cross-country to the ranch. The fence line seemed to go on forever, heat bearing down on her, dry wind pulling and pressing. Maybe it was luck or fate, maybe sheer determination, but she found the gate and rode through. The woman and her father were mustering by chopper and motorbike when Alienor arrived. Paramedics and police came soon after. Blood tests confirmed the virus, and she was told she would be laid up for another two months.

No. That will not do. I need to be back out there. I need my horses, left in a paddock with strangers, missing me as I miss them. I need to be back on the trail. I need to finish this. If I owe it to myself, I owe it to them too. □

In 2017, Alienor Le Gouvello concluded her year-long journey through the Australian bush, accompanied by three wild horses—a journey of 5,330 kilometers. She became the second woman to complete the Bicentennial National Trail and the only person to do so with the same horses from beginning to end.

Ebb and Flow

In 2015, photographer Jody MacDonald was sailing on an 18-meter (60-foot) catamaran, *Discovery*. Her mission: wandering the world since 2005 on a series of blue-water kitesurfing and surfing journeys, seeking remote wind and waves. She had circled the planet twice. Expedition Cabrinha Quest was her answer to quenching an insatiable need for adventure and exploration. Now Jody was on her way to a remote area of the Society Islands to meet up with renowned surfer and explorer Liz Clark and her boat *Swell*.

LOCATION: **SOUTH PACIFIC OCEAN**

> "She immersed herself in the culture and wilderness of the outer islands and atolls: sailing, writing, reading, constantly finding ways to reduce her carbon footprint."

Liz, well known in the adventure community, is part of an all-star cast of explorers famous only on the fringe. *National Geographic* recognized her as Adventurer of the Year (2014/2015) for her remarkable achievements in solo sailing and conservation. Leaving Santa Barbara, California back in 2005 aboard her 12-meter (40-foot) sloop, Liz had sailed south with hopes of eventually making it around the world. She spent a year and a half sailing through Mexico and Central America before setting off for French Polynesia. Most of the time *Swell* was propelled by the wind. The engine was for emergencies only, and her refrigerator and electronics were powered by a combination of solar and wind power. Whenever possible she ate only locally grown food, and often foraged for coconuts, fruit, and fish.

Beside fulfilling her insatiable love of surfing, French Polynesia's island communities provided a platform for Liz's philanthropic endeavors. She organized local beach clean-ups and spoke in schools to educate kids on the impacts of trash; specifically plastic and how it affects their environment. Meanwhile she immersed herself in the culture and wilderness of the outer islands and atolls: sailing, writing, reading, constantly finding ways to reduce her carbon footprint.

Jody first met Liz in a boatyard in Raiatea back in 2008. Boats are in constant need of maintenance and repairs and Liz was covered in oil and grease and caulk, performing a refit on her cherished vessel. It takes a huge leap of faith and an enormous amount of confidence to set off by sail around the world. A lot of people have the dream, but how many actually go for it? A miniscule number—and in 2008 there was only one woman doing it alone: Liz. Jody had known their paths would cross again.

Discovery entered the calmer waters of an atoll, where the horizon of palm trees and turquoise water was more magnificent than a postcard. Jody could not help but think how these islands must have looked when the early explorers found them—but this place was remote enough that little had changed from those days. The thought brought a smile to her face. As the atoll opened up ahead, she saw *Swell* anchored peacefully.

As long as she could remember, Jody had loved adventure. Her first sailing experience was in university when a roommate asked her and some friends to spend three weeks sailing in the Gulf of Mexico on his father's monohull. Always anxious for an adventure, she jumped at the opportunity. Those three weeks were absolute hell. Much of them were spent in a storm and she was violently seasick, vomiting for days. Meanwhile, her roommate's father, who had very little sailing experience, tried to navigate them to safer waters. When she got off that boat Jody vowed never to sail again.

She still disliked sailing. But from 2005 to 2015 she had sailed nearly 45,000 miles (72,420 kilometers), traversed three oceans, and visited 42 countries. She had suffered debilitating seasickness, parasites, and infections including typhoid fever, E. Coli, giardia, and over a dozen bouts with staph. Why did Jody keep coming back? For the same reason that Liz had been out there for nine years. For the adventure. For the exploration.

When *Discovery* anchored, Jody took the dinghy over to see Liz. "The passage to the atoll was grim," Liz said. "Strong winds, angry seas—took a horrible beating. Shit broke down that I haven't had a chance to repair yet. And seasickness!" The correct response would be sympathy, but Jody could not help smiling. They had the same affliction. If you have not lived it, it is impossible to articulate. Then Liz, too, began to smile—because both knew that they were to reap the rewards of their hardships at this atoll.

For the next 10 days the adventure unfolded and they yielded to the simple ebb and flow of the ocean. They freedived the passes, surfed the breaks, and collected coconuts on uninhabited islands while Liz's cat Amelia explored and foraged through the jungle. Waves lapped the hull. Trees swayed in the breeze. Smiles became perma-grins that lasted well past the last day of the trip.

    This is why people like Liz do it. Why they endure. Jody thought that if most people were given the opportunity to live like this they would quit after a few weeks. It was a hard life—the hardest she had ever known. But in time the simplicity of this life had become a siren call that could not be ignored.

    As their time together came to a close, Liz and Jody contemplated the life they were living. Days such as these would be remembered. Such experiences shape a person's life. When time slows down and everything grows sharp. When everything comes into focus: no distractions, nothing else going on at the periphery. Those moments are pure and unfiltered. But they cannot go on forever. There is always an end.

    As she left the protected waters of the lagoon, bound for her next adventure, Jody's stomach lurched. She smiled, looking back at *Swell*, knowing that Liz was feeling the same thing. They would suffer, and it was worth it.

> "In time the simplicity of this life had become a siren call that could not be ignored."

The Longest Train

LOCATION: **MAURITANIA**

"Hours passed slowly and, as temperatures rose to a blistering heat, Jody realized how exposed she was sitting on top of the ore."

Flying low over the Sahara, kissing the desert haze rising in shimmering waves, photographer Jody MacDonald wondered how this trip was going to play out. It was 2016. She planned to spend two months exploring Mauritania by camera and surfboard, hopping aboard an ore train through the Sahara Desert on her way to the Atlantic to experience the country as deeply as she could. But two months was never enough. To know a place, to understand its nuances and experience it truly, one must invest time and curiosity, enmeshed and committed. Yet at the same time one must be invisible, emulate the local people, become trusted and transparent.

Much of Mauritania's lifeblood, its exported iron ore, is extracted from deep within boundless deserts. The safest way to transport it—and to travel at all—is by the Mauritania Railway. At almost three kilometers (1.9 miles) in length, the train transports almost 100 tons of iron ore across a country that has been, like many in the region, crippled by discrimination and slavery, civil unrest and corruption, and endemic poverty.

When Jody was young, she used to look through *National Geographic* and dream of adventures like this: train-hopping through the Sahara on one of the world's longest trains. She had dreamt of oceans of sand, the clamor of wheels on tracks, the cold and wind and scorching sun. Jody tried to imagine what she might see and experience, what images she might capture.

Although the train began its journey at an iron ore mine in Zouérat in the north, she settled on

"It looked an unlikely place to make a settlement, and the buildings seemed to mold themselves to the mountain as if terrified by the drop to the river valley below."

a tiny place called Choum for her own beginning. Yet before she could reach this tiny place, she had to travel by truck for a week, from Nouakchott across the interior. The road could barely be described as such. At a stop during this laborious trip, standing by the side of the road next to the truck, she watched a sandstorm forming on the horizon. It was upon her more quickly than she could have imagined, surging forward in a heaving, swirling tsunami of sand and wind. She could feel it tearing at her skin—and found herself pinned to the side of the truck unable to do anything but wait.

When the wind died down, and she was finally able to get back inside, there were thick shards of glass strewn everywhere. The back

window had imploded. Her guide had been sitting in the back and now had cuts all over his body from the glass.

Finally arriving in Choum, exhausted, she set her bags and surfboard in the dirt and settled down to wait for the train to arrive in early evening. As the temperature dropped with nightfall there was still no sign of the train. A mud shack beside the tracks provided some shelter from the cold, but inside she found only sand, garbage, and the tang of stale urine. More people began to arrive: a family, and a man with a small herd of goats. The family set about making a fire and cooking dinner by the tracks, and the kids ran around, playing and laughing.

> "A journey of 700 kilometers lay ahead to the city of Nouadhibou on the Atlantic coast, winding through vast, arid plains."

When the train finally arrived, a whining growl heard long before it was seen, it was five hours late and long after midnight. She grabbed her gear and waited for the train to slow. It did not stop. Running alongside the carriages, head torch beam flickering on the ground ahead, she had no idea how much time she had to get on. So she quickly hauled herself up one of the ladders to the ore car and hurled her gear into it.

Now long past tired, Jody settled atop the heap of iron ore as the train creaked and moaned and picked up speed. Bitterly cold wind howled through the ore car, and she had to improvise a makeshift bed on top of the ore next to one wall, snuggling into a down jacket to keep warm. The constant noise made sleep almost impossible. Due to the train's enormous length, the cars would hammer together violently whenever it changed speed.

With dawn came the realization that the ore had seeped into her clothing and stained everything—and also that she was not alone. People emerged from beneath whatever blankets and clothing they had been able to bring to shelter them from the brutal cold of the desert night. As the sun gave its warmth, the passengers looked across the vast Sahara. A journey of 700 kilometers (435 miles) lay ahead to the city of Nouadhibou on the Atlantic coast, winding through vast, arid plains. The Mauritania Railway served not only as the sole connection between remote locations and the country's only major shipping port, but also as free transport for locals seeking to travel from isolated communities to the coast.

Hours passed slowly and, as temperatures rose to a blistering heat, Jody realized how exposed she was sitting on top of the ore. The abrasive ore dust got everywhere but, prepared for this, she wore ski googles to protect her eyes and wrapped scarves around her head and mouth. There was little to see other than the limitless undulating dunes, a few small homes, and dead camels beside the tracks. Secretly, she wished there was some respite from the heat—but paying a few dollars for a hard wooden seat in the carriage at the back of the train would make her feel detached from the world around her. Why come to a place like this to lock yourself away in an enclosed car?

Eventually, the train pulled into Nouadhibou, where she headed out in search of undiscovered surf and a huge cemetery of lost shipwrecks. Land mines riddled the landscape; access to the coast was a delicate task. Many of the wrecks were rumored to have been salvaged for scrap, but Jody doubted the Mauritanian people had benefited from whatever money might have been made.

At journey's end, reflecting on sandstorms and train-hopping, iron ore and lost shipwrecks, she realized that in this impoverished, camera-shy place she had found it: one of those rare occasions when her dreams and reality converged and played out exactly as she had imagined. ☐

Taking Flight

LOCATION: **JORDAN**

There are destinations whose name alone conjures dreams in the mind. Wadi Rum, a desert valley in southern Jordan, is one of them. And some adventures arise spontaneously, born from friendship and a passion for adventure itself.

Wadi Rum in Jordan is classified as a UNESCO World Heritage Site for its natural and cultural richness, and the rock climbing there is very special, renowned throughout the world. But when climber Liv Sansoz, photographer Aurélie Gonin, and paragliding instructor Zeb Roche made their way to Wadi Rum, their goal was more than climbing: they wanted to fly from its sandstone towers after climbing them. In the weeks prior to departure, they made contact with a Bedouin couple named Ali and Alia, who agreed to be their hosts. Combined with paragliding training for Aurélie and some research into possible routes, they felt ready—or as ready as they were ever going to be.

Their introduction to the valley came the morning after arrival, and what an introduction it was. Anticipation was palpable as the three crammed into the back of Ali's four-by-four, which bounced along over the rough terrain. The desert surrounded them: an ocean of sand, sometimes white, sometimes red, dotted with gigantic towers of ocher sandstone. "It is so much bigger than I imagined!" Zeb exclaimed. "And it is beautiful."

Superb cracks, chimneys, offwidths, face climbing on small holds: Wadi Rum has it all. Although the holds are quite solid on most of the classic routes, they found it quite different on new routes or lesser-climbed esoterica, where you were never safe from breaking something. Liv knew that advanced climbers, with a good sense of observation and orientation, in addition to technical skills, got the most out of Wadi Rum.

Crossing the Barrah Canyon, they started to spot the mythical routes that would occupy them for the following days. Then they arrived at a particularly aesthetic rock tower that was home to their initiation route. A first climb, Le Bal des Chameaux, gave them a taste for climbing in Jordan: walls of abrasive and sometimes brittle rock, interspersed with long cracks tracing the route from one fascinating geological form to another, all in broad shades of ocher.

And it was no ordinary rock climbing. In addition to the usual technical gear, Liv was carrying her paraglider, Zeb a tandem wing, and Aurélie had all her filming equipment. Although Zeb and Liv had more experience, Aurélie carried herself well and soon learnt the word *renfougne*—to contort oneself inside cracks or chimneys (many of which were too narrow to climb with packs). After several pitches, they arrived at a relatively flat but small summit with sweeping views of the surrounding area.

Time to fly. In this terrain they could afford no mistakes. Even on a seemingly harmless take-off, you must assess the rock formations and aerology, placing your wings in exactly the right spot. Although it was November, with soft conditions and no big thermals, they did not underestimate the risks.

Zeb, with the expertise of someone who had flown from the highest summits of the seven continents, assessed the situation. "The terrain is cramped, but it falls steeply—a good thing—so if we have a little wind to properly inflate the wing we can take off from here and enjoy the descent." Although Liv had flown from many places across the world, she felt reassured by Zeb's knowledge and experience; Aurélie felt the same. The climbing may have been well below Liv's limit, but with flying there are always unknowns. And Aurélie was completely new to this.

61

Liv felt the pressure for everything to go well, and a background tension grew as she tried not to think about what might happen if it did not.

Following Zeb's advice, Liv spread out her wing on the dusty rock to prepare for take-off. There was not much room for preparing the paraglider before jumping into the void. A light breeze from the south touched her cheek, but a few gusts from behind unnerved her—far from perfect. The ground at their feet was less than ideal, too. Small flakes were catching at her lines. She found herself only two meters (six feet) from the edge. It would be worse for Zeb with his much bigger tandem wing.

Liv caught Aurélie's eye. She looked worried. "I have never done such a take-off," Liv admitted with a smile to

"The Bedouin have benefited from the development of tourism, but they also try to preserve the authenticity of their way of life."

her, "and it stresses me out, scares me a little." She did not voice this to make Aurélie more worried, but to give form to the anxiety, remind them all that a little fear can be a good thing, that it should not be hidden away. Sometimes it helps to sharpen the decision-making process.

They had to wait for a proper face wind, but with Zeb by her side, and 100 percent focused, Liv took off like she had never taken off before. And it was glorious. Soon enough, she could hear whoops of joy from Zeb and Aurélie in the tandem glider behind her. Their first climb and flight had been a success. And the tone of the trip was set.

***

Back down at the valley floor, a man sitting in the shade of his tent had seen their flight. He invited them eagerly in to share a cup of tea, strong and very sweet—their introduction to Bedouin hospitality, and the first of many positive interactions with people who had seen them fly overhead. These nomadic people have a tradition of welcoming and helping people in the desert. Soon enough, Ali came back in his vehicle to pick them up and take them back to his camp, where they would be staying for some of their time in Jordan.

They soon learned that the Bedouin have set up sites in the desert with small traditional tents surrounding a communal living space. There travelers can warm themselves around a fire and share the local cuisine, mainly based on houmous, *shrak* (pita bread), chicken, and rice. As they entered the camp, she was struck by how its construction respected the style of traditional nomadic life while being more comfortable than she had expected. Solar panels provided a few hours of electricity. There were even

reservoirs with fresh water—a precious resource in this arid place. The Bedouin have benefited from the development of tourism, but they also try to preserve the authenticity of their way of life.

Their climbing highlight in Wadi Rum was La Guerre Sainte, an arrow-straight route of 400 meters (1,312 feet) and 12 pitches on the vertical wall of the Nassrani North summit. Their plan was to climb this more difficult route without paragliders. Rain all night dampened spirits and resolve, and Liv was not psyched to climb knowing that the sandstone would be more fragile now—bolts would be weaker, and they would run the risk of breaking holds. But Zeb was less worried. After two pitches, they could see that the rock above was dry, and between them they decided to keep going. Pitch after pitch Liv got the flow back and enjoyed the rest of the route all the way to the top. This magnificent climb seemed to get better with every pitch, some of which had thrilling technical moments, and while Aurélie stayed on the ground watching the others through her long lens Liv enjoyed sharing the emotions of this wall with Zeb.

As they descended, Liv found herself thinking that it had been a long time since she had climbed such a satisfying route in such a special place.

***

Combining flight with climbing was quite simply magical. It was hard to describe the satisfaction of flying next to the rock face they had just climbed, looking down on the village of Rum before landing at its entrance. Then being welcomed home by the Bedouin and their children, who had been pointing up at them in the sky a few moments before. The group spent half their time in the village—a noisy and lively place filled with dogs, chickens, and camels—and got to know the people there, many of whom were curious about their adventures.

Walid, the 20-year-old son of Ali and Alia, had watched them fly several times and could hardly stop asking about it. "Wouldn't it be nice if we could help him fly before we have to head home?" Liv mentioned to Zeb.

Together, they climbed a large dune with the tandem glider. As soon as Walid figured out what was going on, his excitement could barely be contained, although he shook his head steadfastly when Zeb asked him to put on a helmet. "My turban will be just as protective!" he insisted. Cries of joy echoed over the desert of Wadi Rum when they took off into a steady headwind, and Liv knew she would always treasure the memory of Walid flying in his *kamis* (traditional Bedouin dress), long legs in his white trousers hanging beneath the canopy and a smile of pure happiness on his face. ☐

Monarca

LOCATION: **UNITED STATES**

In 2020, inspired by the migration of the monarch butterfly, paraglider pilot Benjamin Jordan had an ambitious dream: to fly from Mexico to Canada across the USA, relying solely on the sun, wind, and his own willpower. The dream began two months before when, dangling from a paraglider above the highlands of Central Mexico, he failed to find lifting air and was forced to land in a meadow 40 kilometers (25 miles) from his take-off point. While packing up, he was engulfed in a swarm of monarch butterflies. He lay back in the tall grass and opened his mouth in awe. Above him were millions of colorful butterflies flitting between a stream and dense forest. The blue sky danced with paper-thin orange wings spiraling through negative space. Lost in an endless moment of wonder, Benjamin felt the stirrings of a curiosity he had not felt in decades.

These monarchs, he later learnt, were only days away from beginning the longest migration of any butterfly—over 3,000 kilometers (1,864 miles). The journey north to Canada takes them three full generations, but a fourth generation flies all the way back—to that very forest. Exactly how, across four generations, these tiny orange pilots manage to navigate so far from—and then back to—an area the size of a playground remains a mystery.

Perplexed, Benjamin dug deeper, throwing himself into scientific papers. Mystified by the magic of this fairy-like life form, he began to question his place in the natural world, and became convinced that, if he could somehow tap into the wisdom of the monarch, he could unleash his own true potential as well.

His plan was straightforward: clear a launching site on top of the mountain, fly north as far as he could, and repeat for 3,000 kilometers until he reached Canada. His hope was that by simulating the monarch migration, and their natural form of free flight, he could tap into some wavelength that would open his eyes to their ancient wisdom. But a paragliding expedition of this magnitude had never been attempted.

Paragliders require consistent weather to fly cross-country—and North America's weather is anything but that.

With his paraglider, camping gear, and enough peanut butter for two weeks, Benjamin stood atop a dry mountain just north of a six-meter (20-foot) iron fence marking the Mexican border. He checked his straps, faced his wing, closed his eyes, and counted to three. His kite popped up with enthusiasm, and a strong thermic cycle lifted his body before he even had a chance to turn around. War drums beat in his head. There would be no meters lost, no thermal spared.

Spinning desperately around a tiny column of rising air, each moment of climbing lessened the anxiety brought on by the cactus fields below. After an hour, he was still only 200 meters (656 feet) above launch. He closed his eyes, trying to feel the air. And then his climb suddenly accelerated—reaching 3,000 meters (9,843 feet), then 5,200 meters (17,060 feet), higher than he had ever been.

Benjamin skipped northward as his luck continued. But, after landing outside the abandoned mining town of Winkelman, progress stalled.

"Unless something changed, he knew that he could not complete this journey—and hopes of unearthing some nugget of ancient wisdom were evaporating in the searing desert heat."

His improvised launch was a painstakingly cleared dirt patch amongst cacti, 300 meters (984 feet) above an old copper refinery. And, after a week of relentless heat, he was still there. Each evening he hiked back up the mountain with extra water. Mornings were spent rationing water and playing his travel banjo under a shade structure he had crafted from cacti. He spent his afternoons getting aloft—and then invariably landing in the cacti immediately below. Without desert flying experience, he could not grasp why he was unable to find the thermic lift he needed. And, too proud to ask the local Facebook group for guidance, he remained stuck in a maddening loop.

Delirious, he glanced at his watch and realized that it was already May 15. Having used up 25 percent of the flyable season, he had covered just 10 percent of his route. Unless something changed, he knew that he could not complete this journey—and hopes of unearthing some nugget of ancient wisdom were evaporating in the searing desert heat. The sun was rising. Benjamin shuffled out of his tent, pitched near the 3,400-meter (11,155-foot) summit of Monroe Peak, Utah. After two months of negotiating short ranges, flats, and odd bumps, he now stood at the southern end of a series of expansive mountain ranges, and the birthplace of some of the longest flights in the USA.

Other pilots waited at this launch to fly. A healthy sense of competition filled the air. Some locals launched with the first thermic cycles, but Benjamin waited half an hour for the thermal tops to rise. Then he quickly ascended to 4,000 meters (13,123 feet) and began the first of many tailwind transitions into the north. To his surprise, another pilot dared to join him on this one-way journey. Both flying wings of similar performance, they leapfrogged forward amongst the rough thermals, drifting heavily in the strong southern breeze. Sometimes Benjamin found the climb; sometimes it was the other pilot's turn.

Another pass and he glanced back to see his wingman gaining in a steady climb about two kilometers (1.2 miles) behind him.

He reverted back north and flew like a banshee—but the low windswept ridges sucked him in like a butterfly in a wind tunnel. Ground speed clocking negative rates, he touched down while flying backwards in a canyon east of the town of Salina, covering about 50 kilometers (31 miles) in all. Exhausted, Benjamin peered up to see the other pilot, still high. That evening he would learn that the other pilot had flown almost four times further. Only a third of the way into his journey, he was still far behind schedule.

That night Benjamin tossed and turned, playing out scenarios in his head. Did he walk north to his next launch, committing to the idea that his best was not as good as he thought it was, or did he walk back south and fly from the same peak once again, hoping to elevate his place amongst his paragliding peers? Walking north felt like resigning himself to the fact that he could not do any better, but walking south proved how badly he needed to appear better than he was. Neither felt right.

The next morning, unable to measure the mighty weight of either scenario, and with some hesitation, he began walking north. New blisters after 20 kilometers (12 miles) were a small token of the pain wreaking havoc within. Two days of asphalt passed below him.

While bushwhacking up the west face of Salt Creek Peak, he turned to witness the elevation he had gained so far and felt a tingle of excitement for what the next day might have in store. The sorrow of the day before seemed inexplicable now—and he began to feel a new lightness growing within him, as if he was shedding a layer of skin he had not even realized he had been carrying around.

***

The next flight north, toward Salt Lake City, was one of the most satisfying and rewarding of his life. Certain at last that he had made the right choice in walking north, shame and humiliation were the next layers to be torn away in the thin air. He bounced between mountain and cloud and could feel that his difficult choice to walk north had triggered his own human metamorphosis.

Four more weeks went past in the blink of an eye. Though only averaging about 50 kilometers (31 miles) per flight, he flew almost every single day that month—and, although forced to walk here and there, it no longer felt like such a big deal. He was now three quarters of the way to Canada.

Each day he could hike, fly, eat, sleep, and repeat. Each day he felt closer to the monarch he had hoped to understand. The monarch caterpillar must shed its skin four times before it is finally granted wings and becomes a butterfly. On this journey, Benjamin knew that the greatest threats to his success had been conceived by his ego. A transparent weight he had shouldered for most of his teenage and adult life, this heavy yet fragile cocoon was truly what distanced him from the magnificence of the monarch and all other forms of life. But, he knew, he had at last shed this fourth layer, and the path before him was crystal clear. □

After 150 days in the American wilderness, Benjamin arrived at the Canadian border: the longest journey ever completed by paraglider at 2,835 kilometers (1,762 miles). He also became the first person to fly by paraglider from Mexico to Canada. The journey was completed without using powered transport at any point.

"Each day he could hike, fly, eat, sleep, and repeat. Each day he felt closer to the monarch he had hoped to understand."

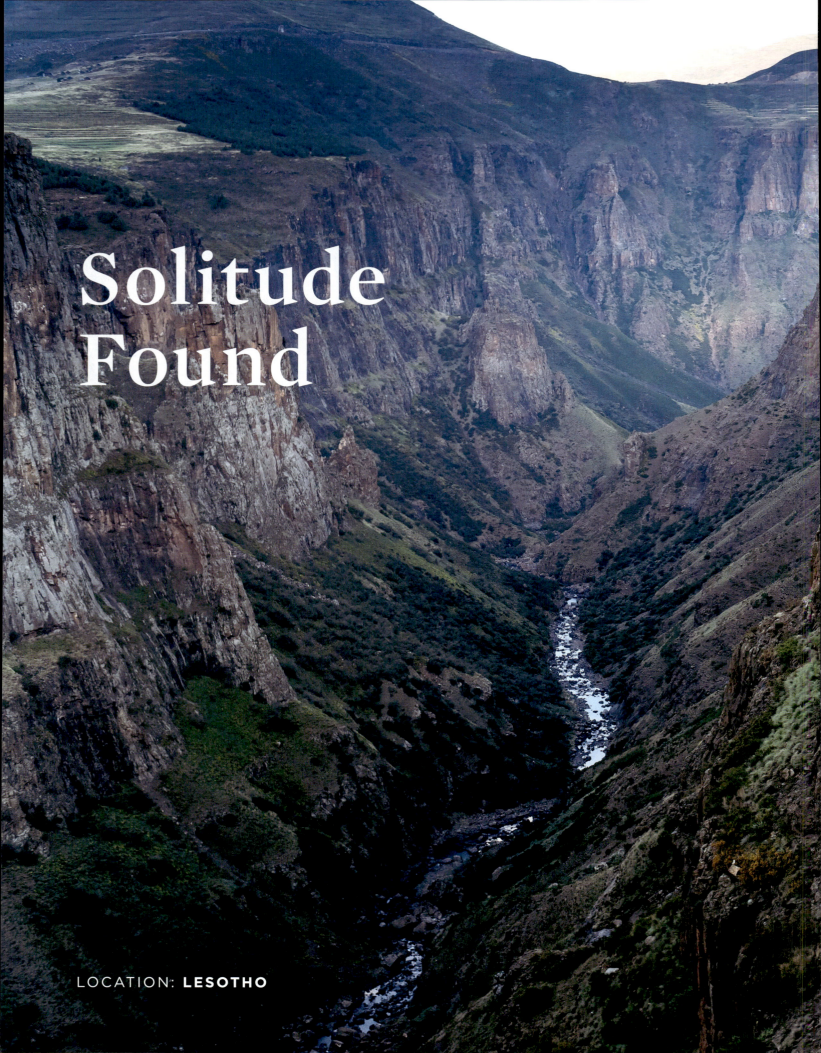

Solitude Found

LOCATION: **LESOTHO**

In our shrinking world, slathered now in online reviews, it is increasingly hard to find solitude. Yet in Lesotho, an African country the size of Belgium with only two million inhabitants, adventurers Dan Milner, Claudio Caluori, and Kevin Landry meandered for days through empty hills on their mountain bikes, silence broken only by the bleating of sheep. Tourism is scarce in Lesotho. Ahead lay 120 kilometers (75 miles) of trail that would eventually lead them to Roma, a university town just outside the country's capital Maseru.

I didn't travel for two days to eat beans on toast, Dan thought. He did not expect to be served them here, in the sprawl and heat of a dusty Lesotho village. On the table in front of him were a mug of tea, beans on toast, and a pot of Marmite.

Semonkong Lodge's breakfast menu had more to do with Lesotho's British protectorate past than the demands of tourists. Accounts said that, if you ventured deep into its rugged interior, you would not encounter another foreigner for days. It was this promise of solitude that had enticed Dan and his friends.

"They skirted the bases of ancient volcanic plugs that thrust upward to pierce the sky, and although absorbed by feelings of peaceful seclusion, they were never alone."

Later, a long way from the luxury of a lodge's menu, they pitched tents on close-cropped grass by the banks of a river. It had been a long day in the saddle, but they were still damp from the morning's unseasonal downpour. The weather had driven them to seek refuge in an old woman's rondavel. She had welcomed them into the darkness of her mud-floored hut to warm themselves beside a brazier. Her smile stretched across a face that carried the trophies of time—a face that suggested few things surprised her now, even three chaps on bikes.

At camp, they sprawled out between tents and gazed across a lumpy sea of tussock grass—devoid of the pylons and street lamps and other detritus underpinning the developed landscape that Dan and his friends called home. As the sun finally slipped behind a rocky outcrop, they realized that the freezing temperatures of night would do little to dry their kit. Aside from their horse-riding, gear-lugging Basotho support team, they had this valley to themselves, or so Dan thought. But as darkness descended, the steep hillsides above them slowly came alive with the sporadic glow of campfires. They were not alone.

Lesotho has few roads; horse trails are the arteries between rural villages. There was a true sense of isolation when connecting these trails to cross the country's southern mountains. The sensation of vulnerability, of being truly in the hands of fate, was almost overwhelming.

They skirted the bases of ancient volcanic plugs that thrust upward to pierce the sky, and although absorbed by feelings of peaceful seclusion, they were never alone. Isaac, a young Lesotho horseman, led them up climbs and across a dozen chocolate-brown rivers. Dan realized that Isaac's ambling pace and unwavering determination to soldier on through, come what may, paralleled Lesotho's own history and agenda.

Lesotho has been independent since 1966, and despite being encircled by South Africa, never bowed to Apartheid. It is also poor; half its population live below the international poverty line.

But it is a resolutely proud nation. And that dignity was apparent in everyone they met, Isaac included. Whenever they turned to him for information, or quiz him about his life, he offered a broad, toothy grin from beneath his thick woolen blanket—the traditional uniform of the Lesotho horsemen. That smile would make any dentist proud.

Hoofed into the hillside by a century of equine traffic, the trail often made for fast riding, but it threw them curveballs too. Baboons Pass was remote, and notoriously challenging even among the most experienced horsemen. From the top, they peered down at a bedlam of loose boulders and readied themselves for a challenging ride—or slow walk. Baboons Pass was the only truly unrideable section they encountered in six days, and it was not a place to take risks.

Physical and mental challenges were interwoven with relative luxury. They dipped into cool boxes of beer awaiting them at the end of each day, and slept on polythene-wrapped pink mattresses—all thanks to two Maseru locals. Thumelo Makhetha and Thabo Ntlhoki believed that the apparent impenetrability of Lesotho's interior was its strength when it comes to adventure tourism, and they had set themselves up to cater for trips like this. Late in the day, exhausted and grimy, the bikers rolled into each village to find Thabo and Thumelo organizing teams of locals to convert disused trading posts into makeshift accommodation.

For the last three days they were joined by Botang Molapo, a young local mountain biker with his sights set on becoming a mountain bike guide and mechanic. He set a pace few of them could match—Isaac's horse included. Claudio, Kevin, and Dan agreed that they had visited few places as seemingly empty and unspoiled as Lesotho, but were acutely aware that one goes hand in hand with the other.

As Chinese investment pours in to build jeans factories in Maseru, it is hard to say what reach this investment will have in rural communities. But that is where Isaac and Botang, Thumelo, and Thabo enter the picture. They know how adventure tourism can transform the economy of rural Lesotho.

Pulling up on the edge of an escarpment overlooking Roma below, Dan wondered if in years to come these trails would be busy with hikers and mountain bikers, all guided by young, blanket-wearing Lesotho horsemen like Isaac. Then, punctuating the days of searching for solitude, perhaps the disused trading posts will have been permanently changed to full-time lodges. He wondered how Lesotho will balance its rich traditions with the promising future being grasped by people like Isaac, and would beans on toast still be on the menu?

Land of Horses

LOCATION: **KYRGYZSTAN**

Ashley Parsons and Quentin Boehm created *En Selle*: a documentary film project exploring a special journey on bicycle and horseback, traveling east from France. They sought to encourage eco-conscious adventure, pushing past limits, and sharing moments with friends old and new. After cycling to Uzbekistan, they crossed Albania, and in summer 2021 traveled 1,600 kilometers (994 miles) across Kyrgyzstan with horses. They had long shared a dream of an adventure there. Galloping across the land. Stopping in yurts for a cup of tea or *kumis* (fermented mare's milk). For Kyrgyzstan is the land of horses, of open steppe and sky, of the celestial Tian Shan Mountains.

"Making such slow progress on the map presented real danger. For more than 16 hours they found no water."

For more than a year they had prepared for the trek from afar, planning an itinerary using maps of national parks, satellite images, out-of-date Soviet maps, and local advice. In mid-April 2021 they found themselves the proud owners of three Kyrgyz stallions. Fidel, the confident and sometimes arrogant leader, took to Quentin. Ashley was the only one willing to handle Tian, whose bright chestnut coat matched his fiery character. The two testosterone-drunk studs took up roles as mortal enemies. A little bay stallion named Chaï carried their bags without complaint, happy to be included in the adventure; he often acted as peacekeeper between Tian and Fidel.

For a country full of roaming livestock, the dry hills outside Tash Kumyr felt eerily empty. Dry gullies demanded time and focus to descend safely. The horses were as careful as the humans, gaining experience in tricky terrain, placing their hooves exactly where boots had just been. They inched forward, covering half their average daily distance.

Making such slow progress on the map presented real danger. For more than 16 hours they found no water. Going to sleep with dry mouths, Ashley and Quentin treated the half-liter bottle they had left for the morning with reverence. At noon the next day, they heard the rush of water, and found that a farmer had pierced an inter-village irrigation pipe to siphon off this precious resource. The horses splashed greedily, gulping it down.

By late July, the bonds holding their herd together felt solid. It had taken weeks of patience, consistency, and understanding to build this trust and cohesion. By the time the sunup-to-sundown daily schedule was understood by all five, they could bloom and relax in their own ways. Each morning Quentin unzipped the tent to a trio of whinnies. As a herd, they had faced downpours, snowstorms, and hailstorms. They had crossed frozen rivers and snowfields. In the 1,000 kilometers (621 miles) leading up to the Naryn River, Quentin and Ashley were the beta testers for trail safety—sliding down cliffs, falling into chasms, disappearing into ravines, clambering over rock walls. They did all this to check if the trail was safe enough for the horses to follow. The horses trusted them—and followed where they led.

***

The herd had reached the shores of the Naryn River from the south. There was a bridge two days east, another two days west—but the route east would add six days to the leg, thanks to another chain of mountains they would have to cross before continuing north. But their bags were light. Only enough food for three days remained. They decided to ride west.

Eagles soared overhead, high above the Asian spruce trees. Below, the prairies were vibrant with flowers. A trail used by rangers hugged the riverbank. The herd followed it up and down cliffs, through forests, and over outcrops.

> "As Ashley looked down into the churning brown water far below, the reality of what it would mean for Chaï to lose his footing flashed through her head."

They did not have to think about navigation all morning. But after a slow lunch in the sun, the path narrowed through the trees—and Ashley descended to lead the way on foot.

Without realizing it, she suddenly found herself in a dangerous position.

Tian staggered, fumbling on his knees, unable to catch his footing as he tried to follow Ashley up the steep bluff. Confused and panicking, the heavily laden horse retreated to the outcrop where Quentin was standing with the other stallions, waiting for Ashley to find a safe way. The flooded river thundered 100 meters (328 feet) below, and Ashley shouted to Quentin over the noise: "I don't know what to do!"

Quentin did not know either. And Ashley had no time to make a decision. No time to say, "Turn your horse around, go back to a safe part of the trail."

Tian squealed, backing up toward Chaï, who tried to shuffle away as Tian gave a warning kick. Quentin shouted, "Move him forward, he's pushing Chaï!" Fidel whinnied, mouth wide open in warning. A log cracked. Rocks fell. Quentin, pressed against the cliff, tried to hold Chaï back with his free arm—then he let out a long, drawn-out "No!" as the log gave way. And Chaï disappeared over the cliff.

"We'll get him back!" Ashley shouted. Looking down, she saw Chaï 15 meters (49 feet) below, perched diagonally in the crumbling shale above a further drop. She climbed up the cliff to give Tian space to turn. The stallion followed Quentin back to safety, but then Ashley heard the crash of falling rocks as Chaï struggled to climb back alone.

As Ashley looked down into the churning brown water far below, the reality of what it would mean for Chaï to lose his footing flashed through her head. His pack would be dead weight if he lost his balance in the water. She could imagine no possible scenario in which he might be able to swim to a bank.

Quentin wiggled down the cliff and whistled to Chaï. The pony's ears perked up, and he began moving toward them. "Wait!" Quentin cried as Chaï bounded past him, scrambling up to the path through broken pine trunks and over rocks. Ashley crouched down and helped Quentin back up to the path, and for an instant they locked eyes. "We got so lucky," Quentin said.

Ashley's hands trembled as she ran them all over Chaï, checking for injuries. He was unscathed, and did not seem too shaken up. But Ashley felt a sick dread. *We almost lost him—and all because I had not scouted out the trail well enough.* Should-haves began playing through her brain. The horses trusted them, and Ashley berated herself for putting them all in a life-threatening situation.

***

Ashley wandered off to cry and scout the way forward alone, and soon discovered what had gone wrong—after lunch they had missed the turn and followed the wrong path. She spent the afternoon trying to banish the feelings of guilt and failure from her body, barely sharing a word with Quentin. But later, as they crested a hill, she noticed a cabin, and turned back to grin at Quentin; Alpine huts were rare in Kyrgyzstan. There was even a hitching post. The universe had thrown them a bone. Untacking the horses, they let them loose to graze.

A narrow trail led to a stream beside the cabin. A natural pool fed by a small waterfall served as a bathtub. Ashley lined up her little bar of olive oil soap, the rough glove she used to scrub off all the grit from the day, and her towel. Then, without making an effort to hold her breath, she dropped under the freezing water. She could put her feet down if she wanted, but she did not. Hanging suspended, she felt the force of the water as it hit the edge of the pool and flowed over her, then raced down to the Naryn River.

When she came up for air, she burst into tears again, imagining that this very water could have thrown Chaï against rocks. How the weight of his pack and the pounding current were stronger than he could ever be.

As she returned from her bath, the three horses lifted their heads and looked at her. Chaï intercepted her path to the cabin to check if she had any snacks. Ashley buried her face in his mane and inhaled; the sweet smell of horse, dust, sweat, and lather filled her nostrils. He stood still and let her cuddle him for a moment.

Horses can teach humans a lot. They learn, remember, and make decisions weighted with care. Mostly, though, they live in the present moment, taking in information and reacting to it.

Chaï was not dwelling on what happened. He did not blame Tian, or Ashley, or Quentin, or Fidel for the fall. He was looking for an apple or a scrap of bread. Quentin left the cabin doorway to join them, and he gave Chaï a pat and a scratch on the hindquarters. The three of them stood there, just being. Gratitude and trust flowed through Ashley. The accident was a sharp reminder to be vigilant on the trail, but it did not mean they were not good enough for their horses. And it did not negate the reality of sharing an incredible journey with them, over mountains and steppe and beneath the sky.

The next morning, they rode on with more prudence—and with more faith in their team than the day before. Ashley knew she had her herd to thank for it. □

After traveling together for three months, across the mountains and steppe of Kyrgyzstan, Ashley and Quentin completed the journey—but left their three Kyrgyz stallions in good hands. They plan to return to Kyrgyzstan in 2024, reunited with Tian, Fidel, and Chai.

Inshallah

LOCATION: **PAKISTAN**

The Concordia Trek leads through one of the most spectacular mountain regions on Earth. When adventure cyclists Gerhard Czerner and Jakob Breitwieser, along with photographer Martin Bissig, attempted it by mountain bike, they faced a formidable obstacle: the Gondogoro La Pass (5,650 meters (18,537 feet)). Gerhard wanted to fulfill a dream by visiting Concordia in northern Pakistan. As the confluence of two mighty glaciers, the Godwin-Austen and the Baltoro, it is considered the heart of the Karakoram. The Concordia Trek takes in this wonder—along with many more—but the journey ahead of the adventurers would take two weeks. And they did not know how much of it would be possible on two wheels.

In Skardu they met their guide for the next two weeks: Isaak, 60 years old with a full beard and good English. When Jakob asked him if he thought it would be possible to do the trek on mountain bikes, Isaak paused for only a moment before grinning. "Yes, it is possible. *Inshallah!*"—in other words, "God willing." They talked to people just returned from the mountains, asking about conditions. The answers ranged from "the snow was waist deep" to "you will be able to bike 70 percent of it". What else could they say but "inshallah"?

It took two days to reach Hushe, the starting point of their mountain bike trek. Gerhard rode through the village on his bike and immediately became the star attraction. When Gerhard started hopping on his front and back wheels and jumping up and down stairs, the crowd became unstoppable with applause and cheers. Five additional people made up their travel group: four porters and a cook. The young men were incredibly fit, always cheerful, and ready to laugh at any joke. The plan was to take five days to the highest point of the trip: the Gondogoro La. To make it

> "What's the day ahead like?
> OK on bikes?"
> Isaak gave the same answer
> as the day before:
> "Too easy. No problem.
> Little biking."

through the pass, they had to gradually acclimate to the elevation and be in top shape before the big day. Surprisingly, the route was flat under their bikes at first. Spending more time than expected in the saddle helped to boost motivation. Around them, the glittering spires of mountains rose skyward in a frieze of white against blue.

To get used to the elevation, they spent two nights at their first camp, located at 3,600 meters (11,811 feet). On the third day they began their next stretch, heading out at 05:30 to escape the heat. Cycling, Gerhard realized, was now out of the question: the narrow path wound up a great mound of steep glacial moraine. They strapped bikes to their backpacks. Immediately, the effort of making progress trebled, but they had known it would not be easy. This was what they had come for.

After a night beneath the stars, they were ready to set out early again the next morning, aiming for the last camp before Gondogoro La. As they made their gear ready in the twilight, stoves hissing and a murmur of voices in the background, Gerhard turned to Isaak. "What's the day ahead like? OK on bikes?" Isaak gave the same answer as the day before: "Too easy. No problem. Little biking."

But after eight hours of struggling and carrying their bikes across a glacier, they reached their 4,600-meter (15,092-foot) camp feeling exhausted. Jakob, hauling his bike up the trail, was covered in rock dust and reddened by the sun. Isaak met them there, looking fresh; when they commented that the day had not been easy, he said, "This is no city, this is mountain adventure." Jakob cracked up with a laugh. This became their mantra for the rest of the trip. *We are not in the city. This is a mountain adventure!*

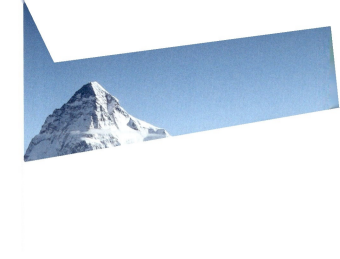

> "Inshallah. You can do it.
> We are not in the city.
> This is a mountain adventure!"

Isaak's briefing before the Gondogoro La surprised them: "Not easy. Little hard. But, inshallah, you can do it." The group looked at each other, feeling unnerved.

Stars looked down on them out of a black sky when they left camp at 21:00, bundled up against the cold and laden with climbing equipment. When they strapped bikes to their backpacks at midnight, they were each carrying over 20 kilograms (44 pounds).

They trudged through the night. Soon ice covered the ground, and they halted to put on crampons. Then they reached the fixed ropes and clipped in. By the tense look between the three bikers, Gerhard knew that the others shared his relief at being attached firmly to the mountain. The colossal weight on his back pulled him downwards, draining energy from his limbs, forcing the thin air out of his lungs.

Inshallah. You can do it.

We are not in the city. This is a mountain adventure!

Vertical sections would have been impossible without ropes. They struggled on. Soon there was no rock, only the crunch of snow beneath crampons. It was an eternity until the horizon finally brightened and the route flattened out, but suddenly there was no more to climb.

Ahead stretched the Gondogoro La in all its white splendor while the rising sun warmed frozen bodies. They poured hot tea and enjoyed the magnificent view, overwhelmed. Four 8,000ers stood before them, resplendent in their snowy raiment: Gasherbrum 1 and 2, Broad Peak, and K2, the second-highest mountain on Earth.

The descent to Camp Ali was technical, pushing bikes through rapidly softening snow in the heat of the sun. When they arrived at 11:00, Isaak and the porters were waiting with cups of noodle soup to revive them, and Gerhard asked Isaak about the final section to Concordia. His answer made them all happy: "Too easy. No problem! Biking!"

This time, he was right. They were able to ride along the huge Baltoro Glacier, a place of such immensity that they felt insignificant as ants. Bare, grippy ice, striated with gravel and riven by meltwater channels, sped their way toward Concordia—and after 22 hours they reached the vast glacial plateau where the Baltoro and Godwin-Austin glaciers met. Their journey was complete. Almost.

***

Their tour ended in a small mountain village called Askole. For three days they stumbled along the rock-strewn glacier with their bikes, pushing more than riding. But on the last stretch their dreams came true and flowy singletrack opened out beneath their wheels, letting them ride once more. "Yeah!" Jakob's cry echoed as he sped down the trail.

Even if this was the most strenuous bike tour they had ever done, they would not have changed a thing. A bike is like a magic wand that helps overcome language barriers and the fear of reaching out. "Pakistan, we will be back—inshallah."

LOCATION: **TIBET**

"One of the largest and finest buildings in the Buddhist world, the monastery was alive with the sound of a hundred young monks emptying from the main prayer hall and hurriedly pulling on yellow hats resembling cockerels' combs. They formed a circle in the courtyard and, following the lead of the master lama, began to sway in unison, booming out the words of sacred texts."

A cornerstone of Buddhist life, the kora is an act of devotion carried out day and night across the Himalayas. Tibetans perform circular pilgrimages around their most sacred sites, spinning prayer wheels and thumbing rosary beads as they go. Photographer Simon Urwin arrived in Jiabi at the start of a grand kora of his own: a three-week journey on foot that would take him from the Tibetan tracts of rural Yunnan province, onward to Lhasa, and then across the Roof of the World to Everest Base Camp before finally looping back home.

A chorus of roosters heralded dawn in the tiny village of Jiabi as Abá rose to attend to his song ra, lighting bundles of juniper in the ceremonial clay oven as an offering to the mountain gods. "This keeps the rains coming and the fields fertile," he announced confidently before heading off to complete his morning kora.

An hour passed. Abá returned just as the sun climbed over the high peaks, warming the valley below. From the roof of Abá's house, Simon sat and watched the simple rhythm of village life gently unfold. Cattle were milked and chickens fed. Sheaves of barley were cut to mill into bread flour or distil into *ará*, the local firewater. It was a place rich in tradition and superstition, where villagers took great care not to raise their voices as they went about their daily industry for fear of disturbing the malevolent, serpentine spirits said to inhabit the fields. Then, come nightfall, they locked their doors firmly against the chill, mindful that this was the time when the wandering souls of the dead came looking for a new home.

The road leaving Jiabi followed the muddy Yangtze before veering off toward the borderlands of Sichuan, Yunnan, and Tibet, the treeline slowly disappearing as the altitude increased and herds of sharp-horned yak appeared on the horizon. Icons of the high plateau, yaks are revered beasts of burden that have played a central role in Tibetan culture for well over 2,000 years. Nomads set fires with their dung, knit tents with their hair, and cherish the milk of the female *dri*, which is laboriously churned into butter in ornate *mdong mo*.

On the approach to Xianggelila, Simon came across Lamu, a Khampa ethnic herder, who invited him into her stockade for a cup of *po cha*—which she assured him is good for hydration and energy at high altitude. He studied the soapy concoction of yak butter, tea leaves, salt, and soda, and drank it. She momentarily disappeared, then returned with a pungent block of butter kept safe for special occasions. "This one I only use for filling butter lamps when I get to the monastery," she said, cutting off a generous square and wrapping it in brown paper. With a smile, she handed over this valuable and generous gift, and wished him well on his journey ahead.

The imposing sight of the Potala Palace—the former residence of the exiled Dalai Lama—marked Simon's arrival into Lhasa. Once known as the Forbidden City, to Simon it now felt unmistakably Chinese, with red lanterns and neon signs in Mandarin incongruously lining the streets. The atmospheric Barkhor was one area of Lhasa to have at least partially resisted the invasion of the modern world. Throngs of worshippers polished the flagstones with their footsteps, some fully prostrate as they circled the Jokhang Temple on the city's most hallowed pilgrimage route. "The Buddha always walked clockwise, so we are following our god," a local man told Simon as he joined the multitude. "The kora we follow also represents the circle of life. Where you start is where you end, so if you do good things, you will get good fruits."

From Lhasa Simon headed south on vertiginous roads, rounding Yamdrok-tso, one of Tibet's holiest lakes, its waters dazzling turquoise, its shoreline flecked with dwellings draped in colorful prayer flags. The most prevalent was the *lungta*, or Wind Horse, said to spread compassion and well-being with every flutter of its mantra, and marked with a steed bearing the burning jewel of enlightenment on its back. In one house he met an industrious old man hand-printing flags on woodblocks stained with centuries of ink. This process is believed to increase their potency.

"The Wind Horse represents good fortune," he said as he hung fresh rectangles of cotton out to dry. "The flag fades and dissolves in the sun and on the wind, and when its spirit touches you, good opportunities will come your way."

Simon passed through the old fortress town of Gyantse, and crossed long stretches of harsh, inhospitable terrain before arriving, as dusk overwhelmed daylight, into Shigatse, home of the sprawling Tashilhunpo. One of the largest and finest buildings in the Buddhist world, the monastery was alive with the sound of a hundred young monks emptying from the main prayer hall and hurriedly pulling on yellow hats resembling cockerels' combs. They formed a circle in the courtyard and, following the lead of the master lama, began to sway in unison, booming out the words of sacred texts. Powerful chanting reverberated around stone walls and trembled in Simon's torso. Night had already fallen by the time their profoundly affecting music reached its crescendo.

He continued westward, the elevation steepening further, the road snaking wildly toward the foot of the Great Himalayan Range where heavy cloud and swirling snow obscured Everest from view. Close to Base Camp at Rongbuk, the highest monastery in the world, he refueled guttering altar lamps with his yak butter to symbolically mark the nearing of journey's end. Sleep was impossible in the biting cold, so the next morning, well before dawn, he climbed up beyond the monastery walls and waited. Slowly the outline of Chomolungma—the "beautiful queen" as Tibetans know her—began to emerge from the shadows. Then, moments later, her north face was revealed in all its glory, the looming peak magically bathed in the first rays of morning sun.

His kora was complete. ◻

Colors in the Cold

LOCATION: **INDIA**

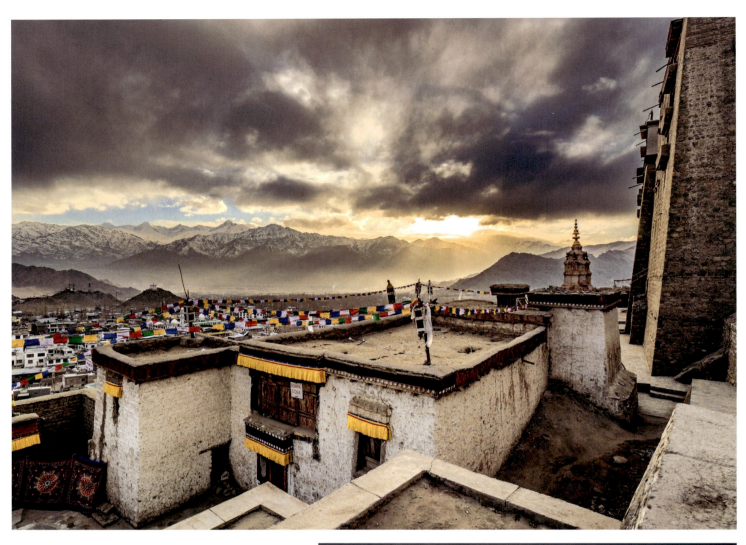

"It looked an unlikely place to make a settlement, and the buildings seemed to mold themselves to the mountain as if terrified by the drop to the river valley below."

Accompanied by a group of friends, a local guide, and porters, adventure photographer Bertrand Carlier's objective was to trek the frozen Zanskar River in Ladakh, northern India. Every year, the Zanskar River freezes, creating the only viable thoroughfare for the villages in this region. The steep mountains are shrouded in snow, blocking any other way in or out. With no road, villagers undertake the trek to Leh on ribbons of thick blue ice, snaking for over 100 kilometers (62 miles) between the Zanskar Mountains. Bertrand and his group included Amandine Baumert—a veterinary surgeon—with her paraglider, hoping to do some flying. Trekking with boots and microspikes over the ice, and with the essential help of porters, they pulled their loads in pulks weighing 25 kilograms (55 pounds) each, laden down by the ski equipment they planned to use for their return trip to Leh.

Swirls of glistening snow funneled through the scarped passages of Lingshet village, where a sinister wind lashed against wooden doors barricaded against winter's fury. Fireplaces flickered in the windows of the angular white buildings. From their approach below, the village appeared huddled on the steep mountain slope, inexplicably surviving the hostile Himalayan winter. It looked an unlikely place to make a settlement, and the buildings seemed to cling to the mountain as if terrified by the drop to the river valley below. With wind-chill it was at least −20 degrees Celsius (−4 degrees Fahrenheit) and the high winds made their trek temporarily impossible.

"In some places, the colors woven into the ice were incredible and surprising; in others, the ice was so clear that it was hard to trust."

In stark contrast to the hostile weather, the people of Lingshet embraced the team with warm hospitality. It did not take long before they were settled indoors with hot drinks and food, while the storm hammered at doors and shuttered windows.

They knew they would be stuck there for at least another day.

Stuck is perhaps the wrong word for their situation. Equipped with only his camera, Bertrand separated from the group and immersed himself in the village. In the snowstorm, its white buildings almost receded into the mountains, but the crimson robes, vibrant prayer flags, and immaculate golden *stupas* (reliquaries) of the monastery pulled him in.

Sitting next to the stove in the monastery's kitchen, warming his hands with a cup of chai tea, Bertrand kept one of the monks company. With the land blanketed in thick snow, people were less busy and had more time to meet, talk, and share a pot of tea. In such isolated Himalayan villages, time takes on a different notion. Winter forces a hiatus of normal activity, sending the population into a state of near-hibernation. Few foreigners visit during these months, and yet Betrand and his group received generous welcomes in every village they passed through. The snowstorm raging outside created the perfect opportunity for them to spend more time with the curious and warm-hearted locals. Bertrand took photos and drank more chai, grateful to be stuck.

After three days and nights in Lingshet, the howl of the wind settled down to a gentle purr. Betrand and his team were no longer stuck, but they did not leave Lingshet in a rush—with clearer weather there was one more thing to do. The children of the village giggled and cheered as Amandine filled her paraglider and began her take-off. All faces were turned skyward as she floated gracefully overhead. Most of the village, especially the children, gathered outside to watch Amandine make a few short flights over the buildings.

After the sky cleared, they were able to return to their objective: the frozen river highway. In some places, the colors woven into the ice were incredible and surprising; in others, the ice was so clear that it was hard to trust. Bertrand followed the guide's confident strides on the surface, mesmerized by the clear ice window to the living river. Sometimes the ice was not visible at all, hidden under a layer of powdery snow. This variety kept the expedition enthralling, and nerve-shredding, with every footstep. They trusted their guide to know the ice and to show them the safe path, but it was never quite certain, and the porters broke through on several occasions. They frequently met locals making the journey alone, risking everything with each footstep on the only route to the outside world.

One afternoon, the group came upon a small girl, alone and shivering on the ice. She was en route for medical treatment in Leh, but was unequipped for this trip, so the team adopted her—pulling her on one of the pulks during

the day, and sharing their sleeping bags and food to keep her warm and safe during the night. It was sobering to witness such a small child attempt what many would consider an extreme journey. When the group parted company with her, it was with heavy concern for her route ahead—she would still have to make the journey back home from Leh. While this route might have been an adventure for Bertrand's group, and a tourism prospect for the guides and porters, for the locals it was a challenging reality.

Their expedition, in the end, might officially be termed a failure. The snow was not right for the return ski to Leh, and most of the group suffered from altitude sickness. They decided to make the return trek back the way they came.

Their initial objective was little more than a justification to frame the adventure they really sought, and found: visiting this frozen highway and the villages beyond it encircled by winter. A new road is being constructed for Ladakh. The rural people who once had to tackle such a menacing journey will soon have access after a day's drive instead. Supplies will flow more easily between regions. And this ancient adventure will be but another story consigned to history.

The Dream Line

LOCATION: **TAJIKISTAN**

In 2019, ski mountaineers Ryan Taylor, Elliot Smith, and Peter Biskard, along with adventure photographer Will Saunders, visited the remote Pamir Mountains in Tajikistan. Although Himalayan in both scale and grandeur, this wild sweep of mountains remained largely unexplored by ski mountaineers. Ryan and Elliot had previously visited in 2016. Guided only by dated Soviet-era maps and satellite imagery, their exploration had revealed the extent of what was possible. So, driven by Ryan's ambition to ski the long-anticipated "Dream Line" glimpsed on Google Earth but never before seen by anyone in the group, they returned.

The expedition began in Dushanbe, capital of Tajikistan, in May 2019. Noise, color, heat, dust, flies, people everywhere—it was a stark contrast to the peace and solitude of the mountains. Will felt a blend of trepidation and excitement for the month-long expedition ahead. He had been brought into the team by Peter and had not met the others until they all converged at the hotel earlier that day. This would be his first big mountaineering expedition. And, unlike the others, he was not a pro skier.

The journey to their base camp was more brutal than they could have imagined. An eight-kilometer (five-mile) portage to the dom (a mud hut they planned to use as a base) took hours. Heavily laden horses and donkeys struggled to traverse scree, mud, and snow. It was a full-body experience requiring absolute concentration from every team member, but in less intense moments Will found his gaze lifting to the white spires of the mountains ringing the entire area. It all suddenly felt very real. Their first objective was a line called the Warp Couloir, which Ryan had first identified in 2016: an elegant snow gully bisecting one of the mountains, 1,100 meters (3,600 feet) straight down. Although it was not their Dream Line, in any other mountain range this would be the line of the season. It tantalized them—but also threatened. A massive hanging serac of ice, supported only tenuously by buttresses of rust-red rock, had the potential to kill if it fell and avalanched down the couloir. And they had to climb the couloir before they could ski it.

The team left well before dawn. But the sun was already up, drastically affecting conditions, before they had climbed to the top of the couloir. Avalanches thundering down adjacent slopes made them all nervous. The shrapnel rattle of stonefall on their own line prompted them all to get moving. Daggering with ice axes, kicking crampons into the snow, overheating in warm layers and lungs burning, they hustled for the top of the line. Then Ryan shouted: *"Rock!"* He had been hit in the thigh by a pebble—and had just seen a much larger fragment break loose above.

Holy shit, Will thought as he saw it spin directly toward him. He and Ryan swerved out of the way as the rock bounced down the couloir, kicking up sugary sprays of snow before rumbling away. But it was a close call. *The rocks are kind of manageable*, Will thought, *but if this hanging serac happens to dump when we're skiing…*

Having made the ascent safely, the four skiers gathered at the top of the Warp Couloir. The view hit them all with powerful emotions. For the first time, they could see into the valley and glacier beyond, revealing at last the Dream Line. Ryan had described it as "a twisted, recurving couloir like something you would hallucinate on an acid trip." But now his powers of description failed him. The line was Gothic in its magnificence.

Back to the line at hand. It was time to ski back down the Warp Couloir. Ryan went first, letting rip with raw speed and jump turns, skiing with everything he had, swooping rapidly out of sight. Then Peter and Elliot dropped; then Will, who had the added challenge of photographing the others on the way down.

The serac held. The descent was pure delight. Later, resting back at the dom, Will said, "That was probably the coolest line I'll ever ski. Definitely one of the most aesthetic." But all Ryan would say was, "Just wait until we ski the Dream Line."

"The mountains sparkled and seemed to dance all around them. Energy and motion and so much potential."

A week of skiing—and relaxing at the dom—followed. The week also included 24 hours of sickness and diarrhea, perhaps due to a lack of clean water, perhaps due to their monotonous diet of rehydrated beans. However, they decided to start the quest for the Dream Line about two weeks after the start of the expedition. Simply getting there would be an adventure: An icefall stood between them and the mountain. So they packed food for four days and headed out.

Satellite photos had warned them of the icefall, but nobody had traversed it before. They had no clue how long it would take. Like the Khumbu Icefall on Everest, this jumbled maze featured innumerable bottomless crevasses and countless seracs ready to fall. It could prove far more dangerous than the Dream Line itself.

This is unnerving, Will thought as they entered the maze, picking their way between ice cliffs, trying out one likely-looking snow bridge over a black void before doubling back and attempting another. After seven patience-sapping hours they came to a showstopping obstacle: a stacked tower of ice blocks at the end of a corridor of 15-meter (50-foot) seracs. They tried routes left, then right, but eventually came back to stand beneath the icy monolith. The sun had been on it and Will did not feel good about its stability.

Peter looked back at the others. "I think we have to go up this. I can't find another way around." *Really?* Will thought. *You think we're going up there with our heav packs and skis?* But they had no choice.

Peter led the pitch. He kept his 23-kilogram (50-pound) pack on, skis mounted one on each side, and led a bold line up a wall of ice approaching 70 degrees. Ice axes questing for sticks, crampon front points biting, he climbed well—until reaching an overhang. Peter's skis kept banging against the block of ice above him as he tentatively tried to overcome it. He leaned out into space, calves straining, reaching out with first one ice axe and then the next. "Go, Peter!" Elliot yelled at him in encouragement, but Peter screamed back: "Shut the hell up!"

Eventually all four made it to the top of the ice climb safely, and on through the nightmare icefall to set up an advanced base camp. A vast glacial amphitheater cradled them right at the foot of their Dream Line. Although foreshortened from the bottom, its geometric walls of rock, and the ribbon of snow clasped tightly between them, looked like nothing they had ever seen.

But a snowstorm was howling in and their window for the line had closed. With dwindling food supplies, they decided to wait out the weather. For days they were confined to camp, glumly watching the falling snow and looking out at 01:00 every night, asking themselves if it was go time yet. Every night, with zero visibility, the answer was no. Until at last the weather cleared. It was four days after making it through the icefall, and they had almost no food left—perhaps an energy bar each and sprinkling of instant coffee—and were running out of fuel to melt water. But if they did not attempt the Dream Line now then they never would. Go time.

"Go, Peter!" Elliot yelled at him in encouragement, but Peter screamed back: "Shut the hell up!"

Other than some slabby, avalanche-prone snow they had to avoid near the top, the climb felt surprisingly easy. Now, standing together at an elevation of 5,300 meters (17,400 feet) at the top of the couloir, which ended with a plunge back down the other side to the glacier, they bathed in the first rays of the morning sun. Any warmth was welcome; the temperature was well below –18 degrees Celsius (0 degrees Fahrenheit). The mountains sparkled and seemed to dance all around them. Energy and motion and so much potential.

"Thank you all. This is it, boys," Ryan said, and they drank the last of their instant coffee as they prepared for the line of their lives.

Will felt slow and drunk from the altitude. Perhaps from the cold and hunger, too. His motor skills a little off, he struggled to operate his camera, and cursed when he crashed the drone, which he had sent up to capture Ryan's inaugural descent. No time for mistakes. Ryan was not going to hold back for anyone or anything. And then he dropped, rushing away on a wave of powder and a scream of joy.

Next it was Will's turn. Still feeling woozy, he got into position with his skis at the top of the line, pitched forward—and caught an edge on something after only a few feet, feeling a stab of pain in one knee. He stopped himself and balanced over the great arc of snow sweeping down toward the glacier. *Nice*, he thought. *We're at the very top and you've tweaked your knee.*

Peter edged down to Will's position and put a hand on his shoulder. "What's up?" Unspoken between them was the extreme seriousness of their situation, far from any help at high altitude deep in the Pamirs. "I'm good," Will said after an experimental flex of his knee. "I'll make it down, and then we'll see."

The radio crackled. Ryan's voice. "It's starting to shed. Be careful on the way down." He had glided over the avalanche-prone slab on his descent, but would the others be so lucky? Now he was at the bottom and out of the couloir's fall line.

Before the rest of them dropped, Peter traversed out over the top of the slab and cut a neat little avalanche, 15 centimeters (six inches) in depth, which cascaded the full depth of the couloir. With the avalanche risk now much reduced, the others could enjoy the ski descent of their lives. Will felt as if he was flying from one turn to the next: pure movement, pure joy, skiing to his limit, sucking lungfuls of freezing air. □

Sounds
of Silence

LOCATION: **JAPAN**

"A symphony of sound swarmed around and within her. The mountain remained still and silent yet also full of life and noise. *I'm here, in this moment and this moment alone.*"

Sofía Mejía Llamas, a professional photographer from Argentina, was skiing in the backcountry of Hokkaidō, the northernmost of Japan's main islands. Throughout a few winter and spring seasons there, working as a ski instructor and guide, she had explored Hokkaidō's backcountry extensively—but seldom on her own. This marked her second solo adventure ever, and her first on this mountain, Shakunage-dake. Having toured in this area before with her partner, friends, colleagues, and clients, Sofía felt a sense of safety and comfort there—even ease. She had seen this mountain when in the area before. Although she had always wanted to explore it on her own, Sofía could not deny that solitude in uncharted territory stirred her anxiety at times, too.

Her ski boot popped out of its binding. She was in a steep, icy spot, and watched in horror as her ski flew downhill. The frosty wind pushing in off the Sea of Japan wove through the loose strands of her hair and nibbled at her cheeks, which were rosy and warm from the climb. Around her, the mountains and hills of Hokkaidō slumbered beneath a deep quilt of ice and snow. The landscape was silent yet also alive.

Sofía pivoted on the remaining ski and, with the skin still attached, scraped down the mountain in pursuit of the little rebel. Unlike the peaceful rhythm of skins against the snow on the way up, the remaining skin resisted the icy snow on this unplanned descent, scraping the surface. On this steep slope, she worked hard to maintain balance while trying to cut off her runaway ski.

"The wind pushed and pulled around her.
She felt raw, real, alive."

The runaway ski skipped past her tracks from earlier. She raced by the ski, and a meter or so beneath it made a sharp turn to stop its getaway and scoop it up. She took a deep breath, checked her gear, observed her surroundings, and decided to alter course.

With both skis working together again, she traversed down and around the mountain to a face of Shakunage-dake where wind had driven a greater depth of snow into swirling, sastrugi-laced drifts. Finding her pace, she carved a path into the mountain.

Throughout her ascent, she saw no one. Out there, it was just her, Shakunage-dake, and its wintry landscape. From the forest of *shirakaba*, the Japanese name for white birch trees, along a ridgeline to the snow skirting the mountain, there was a sound to the silence. It was different to the other seasons. Winter and the start of spring are so still. Simultaneously void and so full of life.

In the silence, time expanded. In Spanish, they say, *"El tiempo se dilata."* It was as if time had stopped, lingered, dilated. Hollow yet also inhabited. The trees and branches were bare. The mountain was covered in snow. The sound of silence was that of the breeze or the wind. It was her breath, simultaneously outside her and within her. It was her skins grazing the snow as she made her way up the mountain. It was the heels of her boots tapping the backs of her bindings with every forward movement.

Every sound within this silence was a reaction to something natural happening: the breeze tickling the trees, ice falling to the ground, the wind sweeping snow across the vast landscape. It was the sound of things that lived and breathed, quietly and boldly, of things that simply were.

The sound of silence was a hollowness full of so many things, but, at the same time, it was almost too loud.

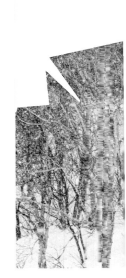

How was that even possible? Sofía did not know, but out there, she felt the truth of it. The sound of silence was empty yet full.

In the shirakaba forest, the silence danced vibrantly in the quiet, bright light that shone between the white birch trees. Japan has an incredible natural light. In this forest, it felt as though it wove through a golden-orange filter before reaching Sofía.

She left the ridgeline forest and started skinning across a plateau. Beyond the protection of the trees, the wind grew stronger, bringing clouds from the northwest that could threaten her summit goal.

Sofía studied the conditions and held court with herself. Unlike past experiences, she had no one else with whom to discuss, make decisions, and act. She had covered two thirds of the mountain with one third remaining to reach the summit. Considering her location, the weather, and how far she had to go to ascend and descend, she chose to press on. She wanted to prove to herself that she could do this on her own, yet also felt that she knew when that desire turns to pride and stupidity—and she was not there.

The wind pushed and pulled around her. She felt raw, real, alive. This island was a place of deep peace and magic for her, especially during the winter and early spring. Her solitude evoked some fear and anxiety but also, as she approached the summit, a sense of freedom, confidence, and relief.

She kept her pace. Her breathing grew heavier, deeper. Though exhausted and a bit anxious, her joy at seeing this summit on her own carried her the final few steps. Wind pummeled her at the summit. Snow flew with it from the northwest, pinching and scouring her face. Sofía momentarily breathed in the view of the mountains that surrounded her and the sea beyond.

I made it. I'm here. She could not help but smile. Relief swam through her. *I can do this by myself, and I should do it more often.* A symphony of sound swarmed around and within her. The mountain remained still and silent yet also full of life and noise. *I'm here, in this moment and this moment alone.* □

Kingdom of Spirits

LOCATION: **GREENLAND**

"For the Inuit everything has an *Anirniq*, a soul."

The schooner Opal sailed from Constable Pynt, Greenland, through Hurry Fjord in the direction of Ittoqqortoormiit. Aboard Opal were Captain Heimir Harðarson, travel writer Marco Barneveld, and photographer René Koster. Their goal during this brief Arctic summer: to explore Scoresbysund, a fjord system 350 kilometers (217 miles) long, accessible for only three months of the year. From October to June the sea froze.

As *Opal* approached Solglacier, a 12-kilometer (7-mile) long mass of ice moving at a rate of 10 meters (33 feet) per day, Marco heard an insolent lump of ice scraping against the schooner's bow; otherwise, the sea lay tranquil, and Captain Heimir gave the command to pull in the sails as they steered deeper into the mouth of Scoresbysund. Below, ice chunks interrupted the darkness of the water.

Scoresbysund, or Kangertittivaq in Inuit, lies in the Greenland Sea, above the polar circle on the eastern coast of Greenland. Including all its side branches, Scoresbysund is the largest fjord system in the world—and up to 1,500 meters (4,921 feet) deep. Marco doubted he had ever felt smaller than he did at that moment.

The ice propagated quickly. Chunks became blocks, ice plates, and then a majestic blue iceberg loomed on the horizon. The ice was everywhere. Slush scraped playfully against the copper and disappeared under the bow. To their right, a blue icy avalanche crashed loose with a sound like a fighter jet breaking through the sound barrier. "Blue ice is old ice," Captain Heimir said. A thousand lumps fell toward the water, freed from the glacier to which they had belonged for thousands of years.

Ittoqqortoormiit means "place with big houses." Those houses looked like brightly colored Lego blocks, with pointy roofs, against otherwise dreary rock. Marco could hear the barking dogs from aboard *Opal*. Three times as many dogs as humans lived in this place—someone needed to pull the sleighs. Marco climbed into their rubber boat, and they crossed a vigorous sea to the jetty. Seal carcasses, attached to the ladder, swayed in the water below; the sea acted as a fridge, and the dogs loved seal-blubber.

The family of Ingrid Anike welcomed the group. They were serving stewed muskox: fatty meat resembling beef. Hunting is important here. Birds, seals, Arctic hares and foxes, muskox, and the mighty polar bear reside in and around Scoresbysund. Everything is prey for the Inuit. "For the Inuit everything has an *Anirniq*, a soul," Ingrid explained. "Together they form *Anirniit*, the kingdom of spirits. As long as the *Anirniit* are satisfied there is prosperity. But if the spirits turn against you, oh boy…" An Inuit taken by a polar bear?

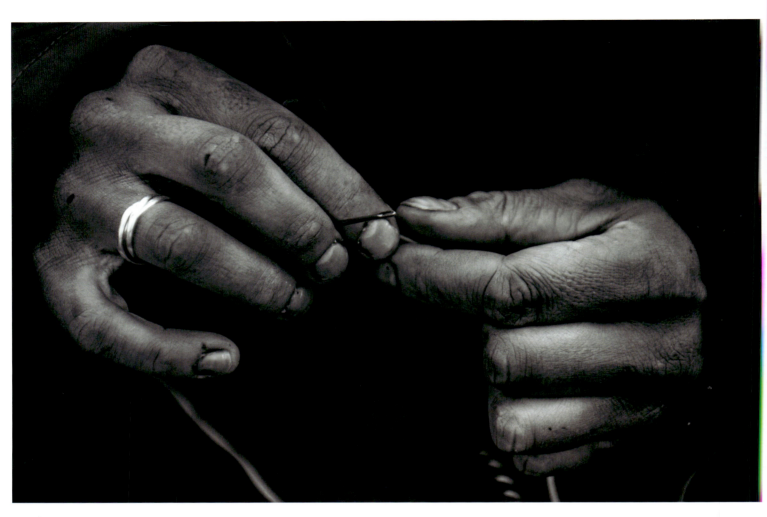

"The world around him was the world as it had been since the beginning of time; shaped only by natural forces and polished by the ice and wind."

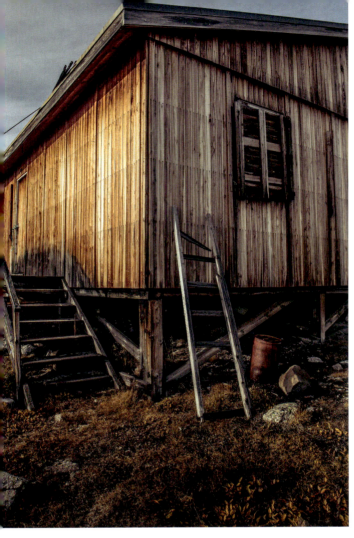

This is the doing of Nanoek, the master of the polar bears. The boy who tragically drowned in the sea a few hours before they arrived? Swallowed by Sedna, the mistress of the sea. Then there was Mahaha, a demon who terrorized the entire Arctic area and tickled its victims to death.

Opal sailed on, into Fønfjord. It was the first time in three days that they were blessed with wind, and not just a little. Captain Heimir gave the order to set out all the sails. Marco and the crew hung onto the ropes until their hands burned and the sails were tight.

Under a cloudless blue sky, a muskox grazed by itself while its soft hair flapped in the polar wind—a survival suit defying the icy cold. Marco's lungs filled with sea air, at once freezing and salty. The schooner's rigging was tight. The world around him was the world as it had been since the beginning of time; shaped only by natural forces and polished by the ice and wind. What to do if you woke up here, on a beach of black sand? Where would you walk to? How would you survive? Even if the cold did not get you, and if you managed to catch an Arctic hare, the chance of surviving and seeing another human being one day was minimal.

As quickly as the wind had picked them up when they turned into Fønfjord did it let them down when they sailed into Rødefjord. The night fell clear as crystal, and the stars in the polar night made Marco feel almost melancholic. He was staring at the star-speckled sky when gusts of light, green and pink and orange, began to move high above. Marco had seen the Northern Lights before, but never like these—so clear, so many, so often, and for so long. It was the first time that he had actually heard them. Vague pops in the night air. It was impossible to withdraw from such a spectacle. Igaluk, the Inuit god of the moon, playing games with his brother, the god of the sun.

Beauty. Unsullied beauty. Marco was too afraid to turn his head to the right for fear of missing something on his left. As a travel writer and an avid sailor, he had been to many beautiful places, including Antarctica and Drake's Passage. However, the waters of East Greenland were the most pristine, most beautiful waters he had ever sailed.

When *Opal* set sail back onto Ittoqqortoormiit they encountered the Bjørne Øer, the Bear Islands, so named because the crest resembles bear-claws from the back. It was 04:45am and the sun appeared in a thousand colors. Pink sunbeams kissed the sleepy, sharp mountaintops of Bjørne Øer. The sea was flat, but made of gold and light blue. Far away, at the horizon, an iceberg the size of a small city broke off. The remaining ice behemoth lost its balance and slowly rolled around, creating a ripple of rolling seagoing waves. Ultra-thin ice-pancakes had formed on the water during the night—a reminder that they must leave. The wilderness was closing up and preparing for the ever-returning winter domination of a very harsh Mother Nature. □

Adventure photographer and surfer James Bowden was in northwest Iceland for a shoot, and five long days had flashed by. After the job, he stayed behind with a skeleton crew consisting of Noah Lane, an Australian sponsored surfer based in western Ireland; Tina Bing, professional model and surfer from Japan; Chris McClean, visionary filmmaker and lover of cold waves; and David Grey, creative director at Finisterre and the man who had put their current plan into motion. The plan: a surf adventure to Hornstrandir, the unpopulated and hard-to-access nature reserve in far northwest Iceland.

Vidar Kristinsson was an old friend James had met on a previous trip to the area. Since then he had become the skipper of a beautiful expedition boat—the *Aurora*, a 19-meter (62-foot) sloop, fitted out for northern-latitude adventures. He had invited James and the team to stay on the boat in the harbor and wait for a window of opportunity.

They spent evenings inside the boat poring over maps and forecasts, trying to work out the best access point and walking route across the peninsula to the exposed north-facing coast. This was where they hoped to discover waves. The forecast hinted at a moderate but short-lived swell.

In the blue light of dawn they untied and pushed away from the dock. Though the cold wind was forecast to drop, it still blew stiffly. Vidar allowed it to catch the sails and sweep them northward across the Ísafjarðardjúp straits. The boat stopped rocking as they made a tight turn into one of the few smaller fjords penetrating deep into the Hornstrandir peninsula, and as the pebble beach at the head of

the fjord came into view, they dropped sails. Vidar revved the engine on the inflatable dinghy, the wake streaming out across the now glassy waters. From the beach they could make him out pulling up alongside *Aurora* and clambering back aboard; he glanced back at them for a moment, then disappeared below. A keen surfer himself, Vidar had wanted to join them, but leaving the *Aurora* was out of the question.

James and his friends were now alone on the peninsula. Looking north, they could make out a rarely walked track following the river up to the steep valley, around a huge granite bluff and up to a saddle between two peaks.

East of their route glowed the unmistakable white of Drangajökull, Iceland's northernmost glacier.

After stops to rearrange equipment and discuss the best ways of hiking long distances with surfboards (the perfect way is yet to be discovered) they slowly spread out along the route. One hour up to the pass became three. Demoralizing false summits appeared one after the other. Finally they reached the saddle and got their first view of the ocean in the distance. Barely any swell was getting into the bay at the end of the long valley ahead.

So they did what all surfers do so well: they made excuses and focused on the positive. Perhaps it was the tide; perhaps hidden reefs out to sea refracted the swell away from the bay. Perhaps it was the strong wind the night before, or, God forbid, perhaps they had just made the wrong call. Either way, maybe, just maybe, it would be bigger than it looked when they got down there.

The trail faded as the team descended into the valley, then disappeared as they reached the sodden valley floor. Snaking braids of a glacial river made their way to the ocean and blocked their route at every turn, forcing them to backtrack and then eventually jump smaller sections as the light began to fade. Finally, they reached a berm of Russian driftwood at the top of the beach and tumbled out onto the gray sand. Their hopes were dashed. It was small, if not smaller than it had looked from afar; knee-high waves, at best.

They lay back, exhausted, dropping into the soft shoreline grass to rest aching bodies. Hours of dreaming what it might be like in these bays; all that talk, planning, preparation, work, and travel, and now they found themselves in one of the remotest corners of Europe, alone, facing north into the cold Arctic sea, about to pitch tents in the rain—and, hopefully, to surf. A questionable pursuit.

Soon enough they coaxed a driftwood fire to life as the world of light shrank. Flames offered primeval comfort and warm rations nourished them. James walked off up the beach alone to fill water bottles from the river, turning off his head lamp as he left the fire and storytelling behind him.

"Finally, they reached a berm of Russian driftwood at the top of the beach and tumbled out onto the gray sand. Their hopes were dashed."

It was dark, but a kind of dark he had not experienced before: deep, deep black; no moon, no stars, no horizon; as immense as it was claustrophobic. He stood there for a while, listening to nothing and looking into the black, then jumped as he heard a rustle in the grass below. He flicked on his lamp. Staring back at him were the glowing eyes of a *melrakki*, the Icelandic Arctic fox. They held each other's gaze for a few long seconds—then lights out, and it disappeared into the long grass with a flash of mottled brown, its summer coat.

James made his way back to the campsite. The others had retreated to their tents. He sat by the last glowing embers of the dying fire and watched the wind blow a couple of sparks offshore, in the direction of the beach. Then he smiled, realizing that it didn't matter at all—the pursuit of surf had just been an excuse to take a memorable journey in an incredible part of the world, and at least he would not have to haul a sodden wetsuit back over the mountain.

Not to be beaten, Tina eventually realized the dream of Hornstrandir surf for them all. Before setting off on the return journey, she pulled on her wetsuit, boots, and gloves, and paddled out into the glassy bay. Tina was the only one light enough—and with a big enough board—to successfully ride a tiny wave to shore.

After the long trek back to the boat, Vidar leant over the guard rail and lifted their bags from the dinghy. "Did you find surf?" he asked eagerly. "Well, yeah, kind of," Noah replied with a smile.

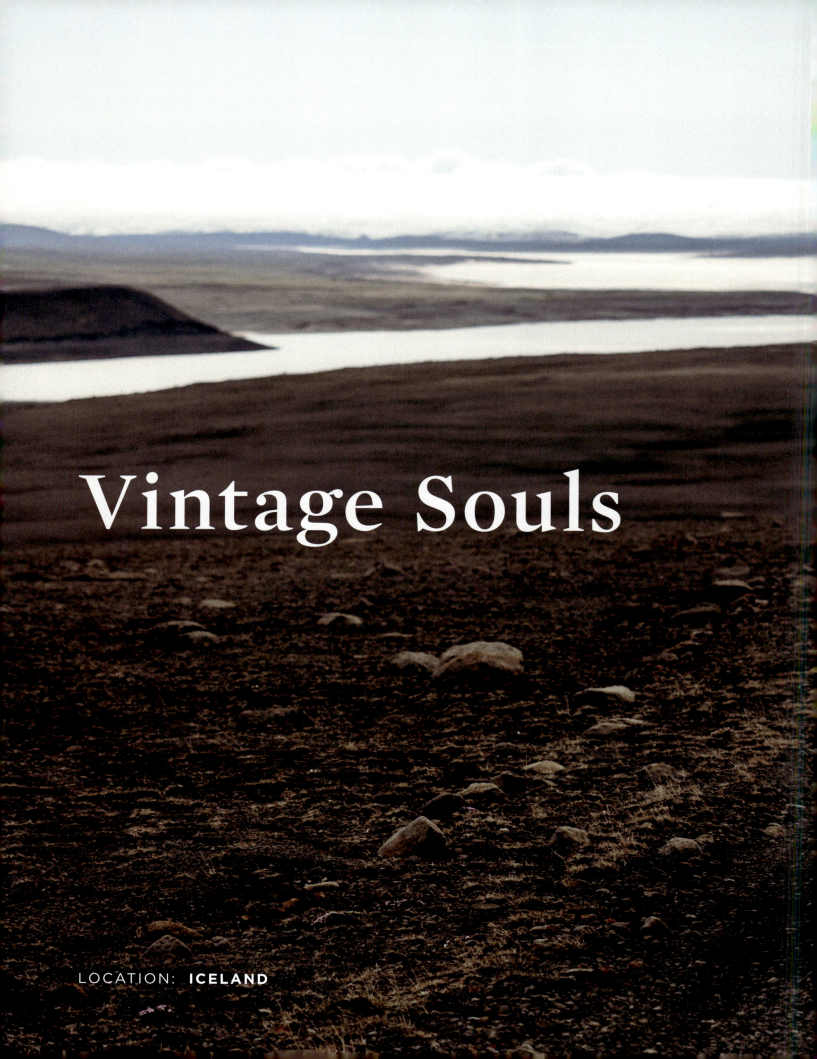

Vintage Souls

LOCATION: **ICELAND**

In late 2019, Jonathan Steinhoff and Alena Reinecke fired up Sepp, a green Volkswagen T2 Camper they had restored themselves, and left Hamburg for the open road. Over several trips spanning four years, they wandered throughout 11 European countries, totaling some 5,000 kilometers (3,100 miles). Fast-forward to summer 2022 when they found themselves in the rugged Icelandic Highlands. With primitive roads and long stretches between resupply, this wild landscape proved unforgiving. But it also offered some of the most magical moments of their entire journey—including an incident that would test adventurers and vehicle alike.

At the last gas station—the last for 250 kilometers (155 miles)—Jonathan decided to top up the big jerrycan after he had filled the vehicle's tank. Sepp had performed solidly for weeks. Despite dating from 1979, the little green bus had cheerily transported them from city to city, mountain range to mountain range, across verdant grasslands and through endless forests. And Sepp had been their home, too. The work he and Alena had done, gutting the interior to create something comfortable and a bit more up to date, while still retaining period character, had paid off. Although long ago outclassed in terms of raw performance, the little green bus had charm—and turned heads wherever they went, evoking smiles and starting conversations. "I remember family holidays in a T2!" some would say, while others would say, a little wistfully, that they did not make them like this any more.

Sepp was sturdy and reliable, but he was still a camper van from 1979. Vintage vehicles had quirks that modern design and manufacturing had long ago ironed out. They sometimes struggled with adverse conditions or steep, uneven roads, and if something went wrong

> "Stark mountains, stippled with vivid green moss, rose like monoliths out of an ocean of black sand."

then finding spare parts could be a major challenge. Jonathan and Alena had discussed this many times as they planned their traverse of the Icelandic Highlands.

They planned two days for the crossing of the Highlands. Two days, a night at a campground roughly halfway, and as much fuel as they could load up. Accompanying them would be Jonathan's parents, driving in their vintage blue T3 Syncro, as well as his brother Benjamin (plus friend) in his own vehicle, a T5.2. Safety in numbers. And the more the merrier for this astonishingly beautiful stage of the journey.

"It changes all the time," Alena remarked after an hour or so on the gravel roads climbing into the interior of the Highlands. The landscape around them was the wildest, certainly the most remote, they had encountered anywhere since leaving Hamburg. Stark mountains, stippled with vivid green moss, rose like monoliths out of an ocean of black sand. Deep snow beds lay in the folded creases of the land, as if painted thickly on this three-dimensional canvas by an absent-minded artist, and meltwater torrents streamed down from on high, carving out channels and rearranging the short-lived banks of sediment. Further afield, the power of change was even more dramatic. Glaciers and volcanoes transformed entire landscapes: the first over eons, the second with great urgency. Alena was right. Nothing stayed the same here for long.

The only evidence of human civilization in this place was the thin ribbon of road. But it barely existed. Just a strip of gravel, distinguished from the sand on either side only by tire tracks and the odd marker.

This washboard surface felt organic, impermanent. Their small tires forced Jonathan to drive at a slow 20 kilometers per hour (12 miles per hour), which made Sepp rattle.

And the rattling kept getting worse. Jonathan wished for bigger tires that would help them go faster—or a better road surface. But perhaps asphalt would be an imposition in this elemental place.

The walkie-talkie crackled, and Jonathan's dad came in over the line, "How are you feeling about the road? Over." Jonathan grimaced, his entire body rattling with the van, then smiled. Alena picked up the radio and replied, "Jonathan says it is lovely. Over."

***

The first day passed uneventfully, save one point when Sepp's rear left wheel did not quite feel right. But it did not develop into a problem and Jonathan kept driving.

On day two, his parents drove ahead in their blue van, while Jonathan's brother drove behind. All was well—at first. They delighted in the silence and vastness of the landscape, which seemed as barren as the moon. Even at their stately pace, huge dust clouds rose from the gravel road, blowing away in the wind that flowed ceaselessly from the heights. Whenever they pulled up for a rest from the endless rattling, Jonathan would run a finger over the thick layer of dust coating Sepp's beautiful green paintwork.

Soon, they began the long descent out of the Highlands—too soon in a way, and yet they were relieved to be heading back toward civilization. Now the

road tilted downhill. A long, steady, 20-kilometer (12-mile) descent back to bigger roads. Which is when that rear left wheel started to feel wrong again whenever Jonathan applied the brakes.

Then Benjamin's voice came over the walkie-talkie, "Stop, stop! I see fire or smoke! Over!" Alena gasped, wound down the window, and leaned outside. "Hard to see with the dust... but there is smoke!"

Wary of putting too much stress on the already overworked brakes, Jonathan stopped slowly, grateful that they had not been driving at speed. Ahead, his parents' blue T3 Syncro had already stopped, and by the time Sepp came to a halt Jonathan's dad was standing by the side of the road with a fire extinguisher, expression urgent.

It smelled bad—really bad. Jonathan saw the acrid smoke pouring from the left wheel, their beautiful bus covered in grime and hurting. "Oh no!" he groaned. But the fire extinguisher was not needed. With everyone else standing at a safe distance, a quick inspection proved that there were no actual flames. The heat from the locked brake was intense, though. The whole wheel radiated it.

They jacked up the vehicle. The wheel would not turn. "Nothing can be done until it cools down," Benjamin said. "And then we will see what is what."

***

For an hour, maybe two, they watched and waited and worried. The three vehicles, stationary on this track in the middle of awesome wilderness, had never seemed more out of place now that one of them was wounded and immobile. Sepp looked sad and forlorn and dusty up there on the wheel jack.

To love a vintage vehicle—to restore and use any vintage item that has long ago become obsolete, really—is to hold up a hand to the stampede of time, make a statement about what we value. That not everything has to be scrapped because something newer has come along. That it is OK for some things to just be—and to keep on being, defying entropy and perhaps telling us that it is all going to be fine. That endurance is possible. That not everything comes to an end.

But bringing Sepp here, to a place where Nature is at her most energetic, where nothing remains the same from one year to the next, had perhaps affronted the old spirits that animated the land.

"It smelled bad—really bad. Jonathan saw the acrid smoke pouring from the left wheel, their beautiful bus covered in grime and hurting. "Oh no!" he groaned."

Entropy flattens all mountains if you wait long enough. Nothing lives forever—not even a 1979 camper van with such soul that he had become a very real character in the lives of those around him.

Those were Jonathan's anxious thoughts as he waited for the wheel to cool. But cool it eventually did. And, when they tried spinning it again, miraculously the brake unlocked and the wheel moved freely.

Jonathan and Alena shared an anxious look as they climbed back into the cab. "Are we going to do this?" she asked him. He sighed. "What else can we do? We have to get out of the Highlands."

So they carried on coasting downhill, Jonathan squeezing the brakes delicately at first before realizing that they felt fine now, that he could use the brakes normally. After a while they stopped again to check the wheel. It was cool. To all appearances the fault had miraculously disappeared. Dust, perhaps, had collected in the brake drum and caused a momentary seizure, but whatever it was had cleared now.

Jonathan and Alena checked the wheel over several more times, but the problem never reoccurred—not in Iceland, and not for the next 5,000 kilometers (3,100 miles) of their journey. As reliable as when Sepp had first rolled off the production line. Entropy would have to wait a bit longer. Perhaps Sepp would outlive them all. □

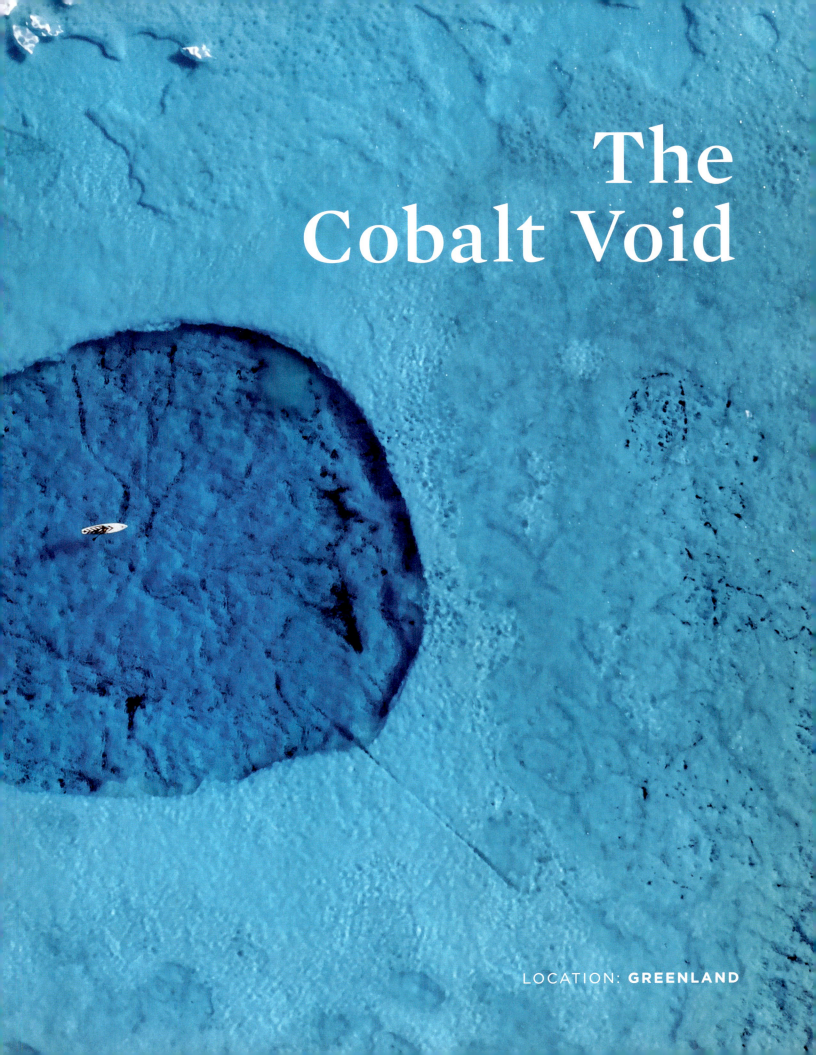
The Cobalt Void

LOCATION: **GREENLAND**

The team of four—journalist Simone Talfourd, and photographers Jean-Luc Grossman, Justin Hession, and Pascal Richard—were halfway through a stand-up paddleboarding journey, traversing 450 kilometers (280 miles) of remote Greenland coast from Upernavik to Kullorsuaq. Self-supported, they had to carry all their kit and food on their boards through the icy archipelago. But the goal was not simply to paddle from A to B. They wanted to climb up onto the ice sheet, along with inflatable SUPs, in search of the spectacular and elusive supraglacial lakes.

By midsummer each year, vibrant blue meltwater lakes appear on the surface of the ice sheet at both poles. They store large amounts of fresh water, but while they can drain suddenly in hours they might also last for months. Some of the lakes freeze in winter while others slowly drain through a stream or river flowing toward the ice margin.

The team had left Upernavik just over two weeks before, and already Simone had formed a bond with the guys. She enjoyed frustrating Pascal with conversations about all the things they did not have out there, like steak and red wine, and they would both laugh as they lamented.

Jean-Luc had dreamed of returning here ever since a lengthy kayak trip that finished at the start point. Although he was the one dictating their route, they regularly discussed options as a team. Jean-Luc was a strong paddler thanks to his SUP racing back home. Thoughtful and kind, he regularly checked how Simone was doing, as she was the least confident of the group. They often paddled in tandem, with and without words—a quiet support.

Days had a semblance of routine to them. They packed up camp, which always took longer than expected, and paddled out, hoping to cover around 25 kilometers (16 miles) a day. The wind often had other ideas, but the midnight sun afforded them plenty of time. With each person carrying up to 70 kilograms (154 pounds) of equipment, they prioritized making progress on the water, rarely stopping for toilet breaks.

> "This hostile land kept them alert and ignited that fire in their bellies. They learnt to be comfortable with being uncomfortable. To overcome fear in favor of curiosity."

This part of Greenland is barren, remote, and inhospitable—the land of ice, the dog sled, the kayak, musk oxen, and hunters. The polar bear still reigns supreme. They often found the mood eerie, with vast towers and gnarled spears of ice rising up out of the dark blue depths, dwarfing them.

Each day brought a new kingdom of frozen shapes to marvel at. Towering slabs, larger than stadiums, surrounded the boards, gently creaking and creeping out to the open ocean. They breathed, dripped, yawned, groaned—unpredictable beasts that leaned and lurched, tipping and turning at a moment's notice. The paddlers crossed fjords stuffed full of shattered ice that they had to push through to get to the other side, always trying to avoid the ones that looked likely to tip, dip, roll, or fall over.

Before departing, they had gathered satellite imagery of where lakes might be found. But one by one the lakes had either drained or were inaccessible. They resigned themselves: they would be unlikely to get to one.

***

On day 15, they trekked up from a bay below the Ryder Icefjord. The steep ascent over pathless, ankle-breaking scrambling terrain was a constant challenge, especially laden under heavy packs. The guys were brilliant at offering a steady hand when Simone needed it—she was not great with heights.

As they tied into their harnesses, ready for their ascent onto the ice sheet, Simone found herself rubbing the tiny brown horse toy in her pocket—a keepsafe belonging to her nephew. She was used to assessing risk, especially out on the water, but was not familiar with assessing risk on ice. The uncertainty was daunting.

"*I am,* she realized, *the luckiest person in the world.*"

They stepped off the rock and onto translucent ice, which crunched beneath crampons as they began the climb. Approaching the crest, Simone scanned the horizon and what she could see forced her to stop. She swallowed—and found that she was smiling in awe.

All four teammates stopped and stared ahead at a vast expanse of blue water, submerged in a sea of white. After so much planning, discussion, and hoping, it now lay right in front of them. Magnificent in its azure tranquility, but here for maybe only a moment—this moment.

In the middle of the lake Simone noticed an ominous circle of dark cobalt blue. "What's that?" she asked, expecting a scientific response. But nobody knew. There was a pause, and then Jean-Luc tentatively said, "Does anyone want to go out onto the lake?"

"I'll go." It was instinctive. For someone who did not consider herself good at making decisions, Simone said it with a confidence that surprised her.

She strode toward the lake carrying her board, sinking with every giant pantomime step into the thigh-deep slush—and continuing to

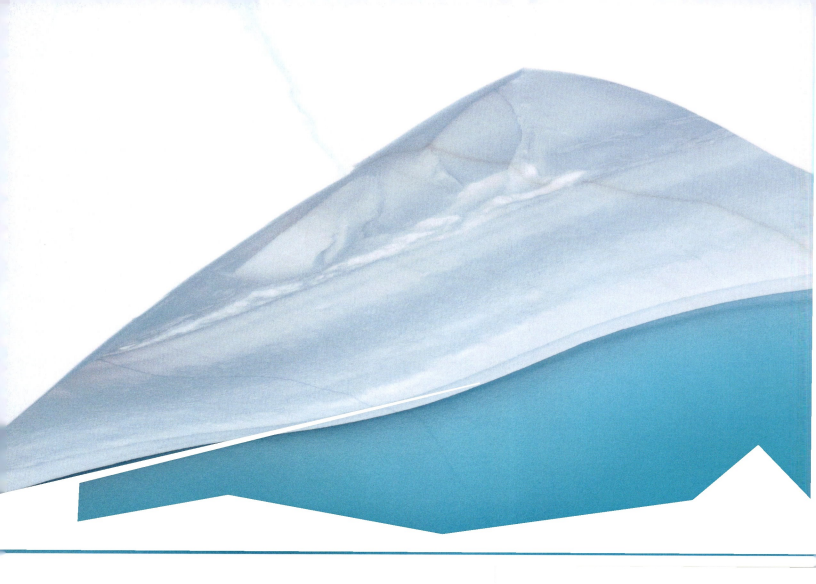

eye up the cavernous porthole at the bottom of the lake. At the edge, she took a deep breath. In everyday life she struggled with imposter syndrome, but at this moment she felt a steady sense of self-belief. She clambered onto the board and pushed off, drawing her blade through the serene turquoise water. Suddenly she was aware of the sun shining down through a gap in the clouds. *I am,* she realized, *the luckiest person in the world.*

Effortlessly, she paddled straight over the dark blue void beneath the waters. Relief and pure joy blended within her.

Greenland is a land of extremes. This hostile land kept them alert and ignited that fire in their bellies. They learnt to be comfortable with being uncomfortable. To overcome fear in favor of curiosity. And Simone continued to learn to find stillness and to quieten the voice telling her she cannot do this, that she is not good enough.

"I am good enough." □

The Four Rules

When planning the ultimate adventure in fall 2021, photographer Alex Strohl narrowed the process down to three rules. Rule one: choose your playground. The Eastfjords of Iceland, with sheltered fjords and rough seas for sailing, as well as spiky terrain with a limited road network, fit the brief. Rule two: choose your favorite toys. *Opal*, a 1951 schooner powered by both sail and electric hybrid drive, would carry everyone along the coast, then gravel bikes would take them into the interior. And rule three: build your dream team. The crew of adventure friends included Chris Burkard, Benjamin Hardman, and Steve Booker. But there was also a fourth rule—one that only became clear on the finish line.

LOCATION: **ICELAND**

The plan was simple: a traverse of the Eastfjords, half by sail, half by gravel bike. Why the Eastfjords? They remain comparatively unfrequented—a stark contrast to the popular Westfjords. The town of Seyðisfjörður, where they planned to begin the cycling half of their journey, is well known for its rainbow sidewalk, but otherwise little had been written about the rest of their route.

The attraction of sailing aboard *Opal*, a tall-masted ship built to withstand the Arctic Ocean, was that the adventure would become far more than just another gravel raid. Beautiful and silent, *Opal* would lend the journey an exploratory flair. Their bicycles, carried aboard until they made landfall, were impressive vehicles too: fast, exciting, and lightweight, capable of carrying them hundreds of miles a day.

Once they had loaded themselves and their gear onto *Opal*, they left from Húsavík in the middle of the night. Morning brought clear skies and an opportunity to view the coastline from the deck. They rounded the peninsula of Langanes, where the white tip of Langanesviti lighthouse peeped above dark cliffs rising directly out of the sea. This landscape echoed with stories of Viking explorers who came to Iceland in the 9th century. Every headland, inlet, and cove had been a navigational landmark for these master mariners. But in 2021 it was also a tempting place for a swim—albeit a cold one. The four friends braved the icy waters before climbing back aboard with huge grins.

Their captain warned that a storm was coming, and that afternoon the wind steadily increased until the old ship's bow plunged into every crashing wave. They could hear *Opal's* timbers creaking—especially the mainmast, which flexed as the reefed sails transferred energy to the vessel and powered her forwards. High aloft, the topsails strained on their sheets. The four friends were quiet as they listened to the shriek of wind in the rigging, imagining what an oncoming storm must have felt like to the Viking raiders of old—or even the

trawlermen of the 1950s who had first used *Opal* as a working boat. The coastline disappeared into a wall of cloud. One by one, everyone who could went below deck, to wedge themselves into their quarters and try to hold on.

The storm hit just before they made landfall for the night. Despite the comparative luxury of traveling by sailing ship, Alex was starting to crave the second phase of their adventure: safe on land, pedaling their bikes.

***

Seyðisfjörður was where the cycling phase began, tackling the southern half of the Eastfjords. They posed on the rainbow sidewalk in front of the town's white church, the rocky flank of a mountain rising imposingly beyond. Ahead lay a long climb up out of the fjord. Sea legs struggled to climb the road out of town, but soon they were on their way, taking advantage of a stiff tailwind to hit speeds they had rarely achieved on two wheels. At a break after the first downhill freewheel, Chris said to Steve, "Guess how fast we were going? 72 kilometers [45 miles] per hour!" And the sun was out, casting a warm glow on the mountains.

The first day was all about stretching sea legs and keeping up with food intake. Ben, who had never been bikepacking before, and whose biggest ride until this point had been 56 kilometers (35 miles), kept pace with the others. Soon the road dipped back to meet the coastline. Although they had enjoyed a full day of fine (if breezy) weather, Alex read the weather forecast with a lump in his throat after reaching their accommodation that night. Another huge low-pressure system was spiraling toward them.

"Soaked through and wearing every layer they owned, they gritted teeth and ground pedals, fighting with handlebars to keep bicycles upright."

"Wind and rain attacked from all directions—a real *Skitta-mix*"

Although they started early to avoid the worst of the weather, day two was survival cycling at its finest. Soaked through and wearing every layer they owned, they gritted teeth and ground pedals, fighting with handlebars to keep bicycles upright—but unrelenting crosswinds tossed them from one side of the track to the other. Alex lost control at one point and he veered onto the grass. Steve shouted something at him, but Alex could not hear a word over the storm. He smiled unconvincingly and pushed his bicycle back onto the road.

Snow showed on the mountain ridges through breaks in the cloud. Wind and rain attacked from all directions—a real *Skitta-mix* (Icelandic for "shit mix"). However, worse was to come. That night, Alex watched through the window of their accommodation as a waterfall began to flow back uphill, denied gravity by fierce gusts. He felt grateful to be inside.

The third day greeted them with a serene smile—almost as if the storms had been nothing but hallucinations. "We should ride a few extra miles to see the sandy beach at Hofn," Chris said as they headed out. Reaching this famous location by their own power, and riding over the wave-washed black sands that featured in so many landscape photographs, was too good an opportunity to waste.

After four days and 414 kilometers (257 miles) of riding, the team reached the finish line at Glacier Lagoon. As Alex hit the "end ride" button on his bar-mounted GPS, he realized that adventure had a fourth rule: repeat. Start another adventure. Because once you start, why would you stop? ◻

Reconnection

As he watched the sun starting to set over the village of Gásadalur, German photographer Hannes Becker found himself considering a question: "How did I end up herding sheep in the Faroes?" At the end of 2019, he had been putting the finishing touches to his van, Ragnar, and plotting trips that spanned a continent. Then, in 2020, the world changed and all his hopes for travel vanished. But, after only a short trip a few years before, the Faroe Islands drew him back. By late summer, during a lull in the pandemic, it was possible to travel—and Hannes grabbed the opportunity. He took COVID-19 tests and drove his van onto the ferry from Denmark to the Faroes. His agenda: simply to grow closer to a place and people that intrigued and enchanted him; and to enjoy the simple act of traveling, in a year that had made him realize how valuable that luxury was.

"The hardships of this way of life fueled the most basic of human instincts: togetherness and mutual support, whether sharing surfing tips or giving up a day to herd sheep."

It was October. Twice a year, the community brought in their sheep: once at the end of spring to shear the fleeces, and again in October, as the nights grew minutes longer with every day. The mature animals were slaughtered, while the others were pastured closer to the village in preparation for the wild Faroese winter.

Each herding was a social event—children were given the day off school to help, and local farmers traveled to assist each other. Every person had a role and their own area to cover. Earlier that day, Hannes had lined up alongside locals. His arms spread-eagled, he tried to interpret the alien phrases shouted across to him as he walked down the hillside. The sheep stubbornly waited until the last moment before hurrying a few hundred meters toward the village.

***

Hannes' days were dictated by his mood and the weather. He blew back and forth across the islands like the tufts of wool he would find hooked on barbed wire or old farm equipment. The wind guided his days—he would seek shelter on the leeward side of these lands, born from volcanic activity and ever since scoured by the climate. Over the course of three months he drove 5,500 kilometers (3,418 miles). He took pleasure in constantly traveling, but never going *to* anywhere.

He met locals in the grocery shops or walking through the villages. While a handful were understandably wary of a traveler during the global pandemic, most were warmly welcoming. Over and over again he was invited into homes to share coffee and stories.

Conversations would take place in English, but Hannes treasured the moments when families would briefly revert back to Faroese. The language was almost musical in tone and pace. So, while he rarely understood a word, he found a strange comfort in hearing the sounds that had a history as old as the first Norse settlers.

Local surf company Faroe Islands Surf Guide own a small shack on the bay of Tjørnuvík, on Streymoy. The twin sea stacks of Risin and Kellingin (the giant and the witch) guard the bay, staring out toward the Arctic. Sets of waves creep past them up the deep, steep-sided inlet to break across black sands.

Hannes soon realized that Faroe Islands Surf Guide was more of a group of friends than a surf shop. Their enthusiasm for surfing on the islands rolled with as much vigor as the waves. They called Hannes when conditions were good and he rented a board to join them. Surfing there was much easier with local knowledge, but it still felt like a microcosm of Faroese life: challenging, lived at the whim of the unpredictable weather, but more rewarding as a result.

***

After meeting up with a group of cliff divers, they all donned wetsuits and navigated along intricate sea cliffs, traversing, diving, swimming, then starting the process again. Hannes stood eight meters (26 feet) above choppy water, watching it draw out and rush back in to meet the cliff face. Then he stepped out. Gravity caught up and his senses were overwhelmed by sea water.

The others climbed much higher and performed acrobatic swallow dives as they leapt, but their love for their pastime went far beyond adrenaline-seeking. They saw it as a literal and metaphorical connection to their country. Playing on the fine line that defined their sense of place, the junction between land and sea. As with the surfers, it felt like a modern interpretation of the historic Faroese way of living, based on the deepest and most fundamental interconnection to island life.

***

Toward the end of his trip, Hannes parked in a layby overlooking the sea, high above the coast of Suðuroy. The days had grown shorter. He watched the sun drop vertically out of the sky, illuminating the sea as it did so, but he was momentarily distracted by a group of teenagers arriving on scooters and parking up next to him. They had spotted his German number plate and were curious. Why would he want to travel all the way to one of the most remote parts of this remote place where nothing happened?

Hannes floundered on his explanation. How could he articulate his time there? In the end he shrugged and pointed at the view, the last of the sun making its way below the horizon.

He pondered this further on his way home, realizing how his time in the Faroes was defined by the communities he had been welcomed into—and how those communities were so intimately shaped by this archipelago. The hardships of this way of life fueled the most basic of human instincts: togetherness and mutual support, whether sharing surfing tips or giving up a day to herd sheep. And despite the apparent remoteness of living in a van on the far-flung reaches of northern Europe, he left feeling more connected to a world that had changed beyond recognition. □

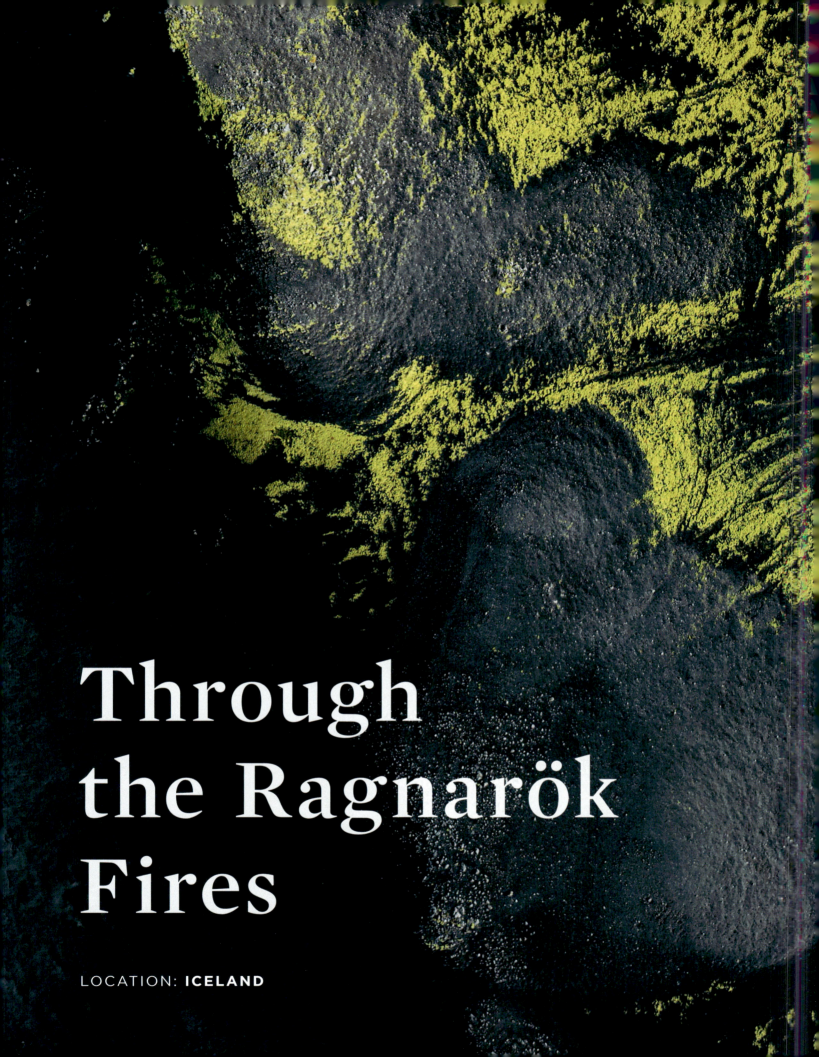

Through the Ragnarök Fires

LOCATION: **ICELAND**

After a summer wardening at the Landmannalaugar Hut in Iceland, welcoming new hikers arriving to take on the famous Laugavegur Trail, expedition leaders Alberto Ojembarrena and Monica Fuentes watched the weather turning wet and windy. Just a few travelers dared to come at the end of September, and the wardens were meant to leave on the last bus. However, they could not resist one final adventure. When they learnt of a trail leading out into the wild from Langisjór Lake, one of the most remote places in the Southern Highlands, they reasoned that they could complete the hike before the weather completely turned.

"Muted gray clouds and drizzle revealed the most bewitching sight, beautiful yet also unnerving: a lava forest"

Now they had been hiking for two days—and a storm was brewing. But in Iceland there is never a perfect time for hiking in perfect conditions. Sometimes you just have to grab opportunities if you feel that there is the slightest chance. It was a gamble with such a poor forecast, but sometimes the best stories begin with a dash of uncertainty, even jeopardy—just like the Norse legends that underpin this landscape. Legends such as Ragnarök, the battle of the end of the world between the Norse gods and the giants.

Alberto looked ahead, shielding his eyes against the blowing rain and trying to visualize their destination for the day: a hut on the distant horizon, framed by yellow mossy hills receding into the mist.

Grateful to reach shelter at last, they lit the paraffin stove, which was completely black with soot after so many years warming the nights for farmers and hikers who ventured into these forgotten lands. The hut was freezing. Slowly, as the stove worked its magic, the small room turned into a warm and cozy space. Monica boiled some water and they squeezed onto a bench as close to the stove as they could.

In a few days a big storm was going to arrive. Even at that moment, after two cups of spicy tea, they could not bring themselves to remove beanies and down jackets. That night at the remote cabin, as Alberto lay inside his sleeping bag with the aroma of burning paraffin from the stove in his nostrils, he had one recurring thought: *This is it. There is no return now.*

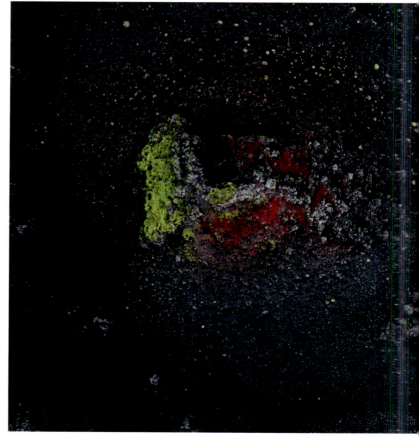

Alberto woke the next morning to find condensation on his sleeping bag. The thick fog that had obscured their surroundings the day before was now gone. Muted gray clouds and drizzle revealed the most bewitching sight, beautiful yet also unnerving: a lava forest, crowding around the hut as if it had sprung up overnight. Enormous irregular pillars of volcanic rock rose two to three meters (six to 10 feet) from the ground all around. Tufts of white and gray lichens sprouted from these monoliths, and with their crowns of moss they looked like the trunks of some ancient forest. Some of the pillars were grouped in small formations; others stood by themselves in the middle of the field, like vestiges of a lost battle. The entrance to this forgotten land was guarded by a herd of petrified *trölls*.

After packing their rucksacks, they set out in silence, hiking toward a steep hill, until they found themselves in a vast area with no marked trails or landmarks, forcing them to follow Monica's GPS. Slowly, the landscape changed—from brown soil and low bushes to black rock, veined deeply where once water had flowed. Then they reached the edge of a black cliff, and immediately knew where they were.

Eldgjá, 40 kilometers (25 miles) long, is the biggest volcanic canyon in the world—the place whose eruption is said to have inspired the Ragnarök legend. In front of them was a huge fissure, rent in the mythic past by the eruption of the volcanic system linking the Katla and Eldgjá volcanoes: proof for the old settlers of that legendary battle. It was easy to picture themselves in the middle of that massive lava flood, standing on the edge of the gates of hell, feeling the rage of the pagan gods.

The duo descended into the ravine, passing huge boulders in the middle of the valley as if dropped there by supernatural creatures. After several kilometers in this dry fissure, the atmosphere began to feel heavy, and Alberto could hear a soft murmur gradually growing louder until it rose up through the ground into his boots. Suddenly they found themselves facing Ófærufoss: a massive seething spout of water falling from the top of the tephra cliffs. After a few minutes gazing at the waterfall, completely mesmerized, they started to follow the course of the widening river. The boulders gained a tenuous clothing of green moss as they walked. After every cataclysmic battle of the old gods, nature found its way again.

***

"Only 15 kilometers!" Monica shouted over the blowing wind. The rain had been intense from the moment they had stepped outside the hut.

Plummeting temperatures the night before had frozen the valley sides, and they tried to thread a route between firmer areas, desperately trying to avoid sinking into the mud. Gale-force winds continually pushed them off course, and they were so soaked that it seemed pointless to take their boots off before fording rivers. Splash, squelch, splash was the soundtrack to their hike—heads down, hoods turned against the storm, eyes focused on the little patch of ground right at their feet.

Hard hours later, Alberto finally caught sight of the hut: a tenuous ghost of a building. As they neared, the mirage solidified and he dared to believe that they had reached shelter. Monica, still just ahead of him, was shaking as she staggered forward, but Alberto heard her let out a happy sigh of relief. He could not even feel his hands, and every layer of clothing was soaked to the skin. Raindrops dripped from his beard. But he felt something unknot within himself as he realized that they had reached safety. They had come through the fires. □

Circle of the Sun

The Arctic can make you believe in magic. Perfect white mountains, with pillows of snow and sharp-edged peaks, plunge straight into the deep waters of the Arctic Ocean. When professional skier Lena Stoffel decided to pack up a camper van full of adventure equipment and drive to the Lofoten Islands from Germany with like-minded friends, those were the dreams she had in her mind. Over the coming days, skiing and surfing and exploring, she found peace in the mountains and ocean.

Ever since Lena's first trip to the Lofoten Islands, she had wanted to return to this magical place, far north of the Arctic Circle. Her impressions of Lofoten were of mountains and ocean touching, melting together. At night the sky would light up with the aurora borealis, a dancing ribbon of light high above—yet so close that she felt she could reach up and touch it. Snow, sea, waves, sky: these were the elements that made up her happy place, her playground. In these elements she felt most alive.

She connected to those elements through skiing and surfing. Surfing waves of water and waves of snow, playing with different boards and different kinds of waves—and also playing with different kinds of terrain in the mountains—gave her endless ways to connect with nature in a meaningful way.

As a professional skier, her winters were long and filled with work. It was tempting to go somewhere that offered something beyond her working winter—the opportunity to surf amazing waves after her season in the mountains and in the snow. But somewhere that was still *winter* with all the wonder and promise that offered.

The commitment to organize a trip like that, and actually drive for four days to the location, took her a little while to muster. But she was lucky to have friends who joined her—friends who shared the same passion and pushed her through her anxieties. Anxieties of a long drive, of conditions that might not work out, avalanche danger, unknown terrain. But she knew that once you make a commitment, the universe will reward you with magic.

Lena and her friends drove through Norway's snowy mountains and took the ferry from Bodø to Moskenes at the western tip of the Lofoten Islands. As if in a dream, hours later they woke to a perfect sunrise, the golden glow lifting out of the ocean behind the mountains and lighting up the sparkling snow on the slopes above them. On the first day they started in the sea. Inside the warmth of the van, they squeezed into wetsuits that made it possible—almost comfortable—to surf in the six degrees Celsius (43 degrees Fahrenheit) waters. The air temperature was hovering around zero, but by the time they had paddled out to the break, they had forgotten the cold.

"The short Arctic day was already ending. They cooked food under the stars—and the next day they started the whole thing again. Surf, ski, reflect, repeat."

Surfing in the Arctic can be harsh. It is cold and windy; the sun does not have much power. But they were blessed with beautiful small waves and sunshine. It was not a hard decision to go surfing on day one. "The vibe in the water is so amazing—a really warm vibe in the cold Arctic sea," Lena said to her friends later. "All the local surfers are so friendly!"

After a morning surf session, they dried off, warmed up, and then donned their skiing layers. The mountains beckoned. Their small group had an empty slope entirely to themselves, and they carved a zig-zag into the snowy couloir leading to a pointed summit. This trace of their time in Lofoten would be erased as soon as the weather changed.

They topped out at the coloir and, briefly, stood together on the summit. No breath of wind ruffled their clothing. They looked out onto the glassy sea and the tiny dotted islands to the west. Tears of joy swelled easily. *There is nowhere else on Earth I would rather be at this moment,* Lena thought.

After taking their time to enjoy the view, the friends returned to the couloir's edge—and one by one they dropped. When it came to Lena's turn, she descended swiftly and joyfully, crossing out their straight-line climbing track by

"The vibe in the water was amazing and all the local surfers were friendly. It's a really warm vibe in the cold Arctic sea."

skiing over with soft turns. Powder sprayed up under the edges of her skis. With sea-to-summit snow cover, the ride took them all the way back to their van. The short Arctic day was already ending. They cooked food under the stars—and the next day they started the whole thing again. Surf, ski, reflect, repeat.

So many moments on that trip stood out to Lena—moments when they had tears in their eyes. Surfing empty waves with good friends. Standing on top of the highest peak in Lofoten on a clear day without a sign of wind, looking out to a sunset on the glassy ocean from the top. Or the six orcas swimming past their camp spot for the night. *I will never forget the craziest week of my life*, Lena thought. *Everything just worked out. I am still dreaming of it.*

INDEX

Contents
Photography: Iñigo Grasset
@igrassetphoto // igrasset.com

Mission Statement
Words: Sidetracked
Photography: John Summerton
@sidetrackedmag // @johnsummerton

Wild at Heart
Story: Alienor Le Gouvello
Written By: Andrew Mazibrada
Photography: Cat Vinton
@wild_at_heart_australia // @catvinton
A version of this story was first published in Sidetracked Volume 11

The Longest Train
Story & Photography: Jody MacDonald
Written By: Andrew Mazibrada
@jodymacdonaldphoto // jodymacdonaldphotography.com
A version of this story was first published in Sidetracked Volume 7

Monarca
Story: Benjamin Jordan
Written By: Lyndsay Nicole
Photography: Benjamin Jordan & Lyndsay Nicole
@benjaminjordanadventure // @pilotlyndsaynicole
A version of this story was first published in Sidetracked Volume 21

Preface: The Journey Makes the Story
Words: Jenny Tough
Photography: René Koster
@jennytough // @koster_rene

Moose Tracks Under Water
Words & Photography: Ian Finch
@ianefinch // ianfinch.com
A version of this story was first published in Sidetracked Volume 29

Ebb and Flow
Words & Photography: Jody MacDonald
@jodymacdonaldphoto // jodymacdonaldphotography.com
A version of this story was first published in Sidetracked Volume 5

Taking Flight
Words: Liv Sansoz & Aurélie Gonin
Photography: Aurélie Gonin
@livsansoz // @aurelie_m.g // alpine-mh.com
A version of this story was first published in Sidetracked Volume 26

Solitude Found
Words & Photography: Dan Milner
@danmilnerphoto // danmilner.com
A version of this story was first published in Sidetracked Volume 12

INDEX

Land of Horses
Words: Ashley Parsons
Photography: Quentin Boehm
@enselle.voyage // enselle.voyage
A version of this story was first published in Sidetracked Volume 23

Kora
Words & Photography: Simon Urwin
@simonurwinphoto // simonurwin.com
A version of this story was first published in Sidetracked Volume 13

The Dream Line
Story & Photography: Will Saunders
Written By: Alex Roddie
@willsaundersphoto // @alex_roddie
willsaundersphoto.com

Kingdom of Spirits
Words: Marco Barneveld
Photography: René Koster
@koster_rene // renekosterphotography.com
With gratitude to North Sailing and Icelandair
A version of this story was first published in Sidetracked Volume 07

Inshallah
Words: Gerhard Czerner
Photography: Martin Bissig
@gerhardczerner // @martinbissig
gerhardczerner.com // bissig.ch
A version of this story was first published in Sidetracked Volume 23

Colors in the Cold
Story & Photography: Bertrand Carlier
Written By: Jenny Tough
@bertrandcarlier_photo // @jennytough
bertrandcarlierphoto.com
A version of this story was first published in Sidetracked Volume 17

Sounds of Silence
Story & Photography: Sofía Mejía Llamas
Written By: Emily Hopcian
@chacay.av // @emilyhopcian
chacayaudiovisual.com // emilyhopcian.com
A version of this story was first published in Sidetracked Volume 20

Forever Dreaming
Words & Photography: James Bowden
@jamesbowdown // jamesbowden.net
A version of this story was first published in Sidetracked Volume 18

INDEX

Vintage Souls
Story & Photography: Jonathan Steinhoff
Written By: Alex Roddie
@seppthebus // @alex_roddie
seppthebus.com

The Four Rules
Story & Photography: Alex Strohl
Written By: Jenny Tough & Alex Roddie
@alexstrohl // @jennytough // @alex_roddie
alexstrohl.com

Through the Ragnarök Fires
Words & Photography: Alberto Ojembarrena
@amarokadventures // @albertooutdoor // @moka_guide
A version of this story was first published in Sidetracked Volume 21

The Cobalt Void
Words: Simone Talfourd
Photography: Jean-Luc Grossmann, Justin Hession & Pascal Richard
@misstalfourd // @planetvisible // @jlgrossmann
@justinhessionphotography
A version of this story was first published in Sidetracked Volume 26

Reconnection
Story & Photography: Hannes Becker
Written By: Tom Hill
@hannes_becker // @24Tom
hannesbecker.com
A version of this story was first published in Sidetracked Volume 20

Circle of the Sun
Story: Lena Stoffel
Written By: Jenny Tough & Alex Roddie
Photography: Iñigo Grasset
@lena_stoffel // @igrassetphoto // @jennytough // @alex_roddie
lena-stoffel.com // igrasset.com
Watch the film at: sidetracked.com/fieldjournal/circle-of-the-sun

Sidetracked has always been rooted in inspirational journeys—telling stories online and via our print journals from those who put themselves out there, setting aside fear and doubt in order to experience the breath-taking, the awe-inspiring, and the magical.

From extremes of human endurance to both cultural and emotional discovery, we present the very best from a global group of adventurers, writers, and photographers all looking to shatter boundaries.

@SIDETRACKEDMAG // SIDETRACKED.COM

VOYAGES

SIDETRACKED BEYOND

A book by Sidetracked
Edited by Sidetracked and gestalten

EDITORS	Robert Klanten // Alex Roddie
DEPUTY EDITOR	Jenny Tough
SUB EDITOR	Emily Woodhouse
PREFACE	Jenny Tough
EDITORIAL MANAGEMENT	Alex Roddie
HEAD OF DESIGN	John Summerton
DESIGN & LAYOUT	John Summerton
PHOTO EDITOR	John Summerton
TYPEFACES	House Industries Gotham (Book/Regular/Bold)
	House Industries Mercury (Text/Display)
COVER PHOTOGRAPHY	James Bowden
BACK COVER IMAGES	Martin Bissig // Pascal Richard // Aurélie Gonin
	Aurélie Gonin // Ian Finch // Dan Milner
	Alberto Ojembarrena

Printed by Printer Trento S.r.l., Trento
Made in Europe

Published by gestalten, Berlin 2024
ISBN 978-3-96704-144-6

© Die Gestalten Verlag GmbH & Co. KG, Berlin 2024
All rights reserved. No part of this publication may be reproduced or transmitted in any form or by any means, electronic or mechanical, including photocopy or any storage and retrieval system, without permission in writing from the publisher.
Respect copyrights, encourage creativity!

For more information, and to order books, please visit www.gestalten.com

Bibliographic information published by the Deutsche Nationalbibliothek.
The Deutsche Nationalbibliothek lists this publication in the Deutsche Nationalbibliografie;
detailed bibliographic data is available online at www.dnb.de

This book was printed on paper certified according to the standards of the FSC®.